Winning in China
— Business Chinese

赢在中国

基础篇2
Basic 2

——商务汉语系列教程

- 编委会主任　王正富

- 编委会委员　曹红月　王福明　韩维春　季　瑾　李英海

- 主编　季　瑾

- 编者　季　瑾　李志娜　李小萌

　　　　柳小利　潘景景　刘海霞

北京语言大学出版社
BEIJING LANGUAGE AND CULTURE
UNIVERSITY PRESS

图书在版编目(CIP)数据

赢在中国：商务汉语系列教程. 基础篇. 2 / 季瑾
主编；季瑾等编著. —北京：北京语言大学出版社，
2010.7
ISBN 978-7-5619-2804-2

Ⅰ.①赢… Ⅱ.①季… ②季… Ⅲ.①商务—汉语—
对外汉语教学—教材 Ⅳ.①H195.4

中国版本图书馆 CIP 数据核字（2010）第 127309 号

封面图片来源：**getty**images

书　　名：	赢在中国——商务汉语系列教程·基础篇2	
英文翻译：	赵瑞华	
责任印制：	汪学发	

出版发行：北京语言大学出版社

社　　址：北京市海淀区学院路 15 号　　邮政编码：100083
网　　址：www. blcup. com
电　　话：发行部　82303650/3591/3651
　　　　　　编辑部　82303647
　　　　　　读者服务部　82303653/3908
　　　　　　网上订购电话　82303668
　　　　　　客户服务信箱　service@ blcup. net
印　　刷：北京联兴盛业印刷股份有限公司
经　　销：全国新华书店

版　　次：2010 年 7 月第 1 版　2010 年 7 月第 1 次印刷
开　　本：889 毫米×1194 毫米　1/16　印张：11.5
字　　数：250 千字
书　　号：ISBN 978-7-5619-2804-2/H·10179
定　　价：38.00 元

凡有印装质量问题，本社负责调换。电话：82303590

目 录
CONTENTS

第六单元 UNIT 6	学校附近有超市吗 Is there a supermarket near the school	超市和机场 Supermarket and airport

课文一 Text 1：学校附近有超市吗　　　　　　　　　　　　3
　　　　　Is there a supermarket near the school

注释 Notes：

1．"有"字句（2）　The "有"-sentence (2)

2．动词"在"　The verb "在"

3．"南边"、"北边"及方位词介绍
　　"南边", "北边" and an introduction of locality nouns

4．副词"更"　The adverb "更"

5．疑问代词"怎么"（复习）　The interrogative pronoun "怎么" (Review)

6．指路的表示法　How to ask for directions

7．副词"就"　The adverb "就"

课文二 Text 2：收银台在哪儿　Where is the cashier　　　　10
注释 Notes：

1．介词"在"（复习）　The preposition "在" (Review)

2．副词"不用"　The adverb "不用"

3．方位词"下"及单纯方位词
　　The locality noun "下" and simple locality nouns

4．动态助词"着"　The aspect particle "着"

5. 人称代词 "自己"　The personal pronoun "自己"

6. 方位词 "旁边" 及合成方位词

The locality noun "旁边" and compound locality nouns

注释　Notes：

1. 动词 "离"　The verb "离"

2. 副词 "大概"　The adverb "大概"

3. 副词 "多"　The adverb "多"

4. 假设复句："(如果 / 要是)……的话，……就……"

The hypothetical complex sentence: "(如果 / 要是)……的话，……就……"

5. 副词 "差不多"　The adverb "差不多"

6. 疑问代词短语作定语

The interrogative pronoun phrase acts as an attribute

7. 副词 "已经"　The adverb "已经"

8. 表示新情况的语气助词 "了₂"

The modal particle "了$_2$" used to indicate a new situation

9. "没问题"

10. 能愿动词 "得（děi）"　The optative verb "得（děi）"

11. 语气助词 "呢"　The modal particle "呢"

12. 动态助词 "了₁"　The aspect particle "了$_1$"

注释　Notes：

1. 动词 "请"　The verb "请"

第八单元 UNIT 8 　请问，林总经理在吗 Hello, may I speak to General Manager Lin 　打电话 Making a telephone call

第九单元 UNIT 9　　**明天天气怎么样**
What will the weather be like tomorrow

谈论天气
Talking about the weather

第十单元 UNIT 10　你喜欢什么运动　What sports do you like

运动和爱好
Sports and hobbies

词类简称表
Abbreviations of parts of speech

缩写 Abbreviations	英文全称 Parts of speech in English	词类名称 Parts of speech in Chinese	拼音 Parts of speech in *pinyin*
Adj	Adjective	形容词	xíngróngcí
Adv	Adverb	副词	fùcí
AP	Aspect Particle	动态助词	dòngtài zhùcí
Conj	Conjunction	连词	liáncí
IE	Idiom Expression	习惯用语	xíguàn yòngyǔ
Int	Interjection	叹词	tàncí
LN	Locality Noun	方位词	fāngwèicí
M	Measure Word	量词	liàngcí
MdPt	Modal Particle	语气助词	yǔqì zhùcí
N	Noun	名词	míngcí
Nu	Numeral	数词	shùcí
Ono	Onomatopoeia	象声词	xiàngshēngcí
OpV	Optative Verb	能愿动词	néngyuàn dòngcí
PN	Proper Noun	专有名词	zhuānyǒu míngcí
Pr	Pronoun	代词	dàicí
Pref	Prefix	词头	cítóu
Prep	Preposition	介词	jiècí
Pt	Particle	助词	zhùcí
PW	Place Word	地点词	dìdiǎncí
Q	Quantifier	数量词	shùliàngcí
QPr	Question Pronoun	疑问代词	yíwèn dàicí
QPt	Question Particle	疑问助词	yíwèn zhùcí
StPt	Structural Particle	结构助词	jiégòu zhùcí
Suf	Suffix	词尾	cíwěi
TW	Time Word	时间词	shíjiāncí
V	Verb	动词	dòngcí
V//O	Verb-object Compound	离合词	líhécí

语法术语简称表
Abbreviations of grammatical terms

缩写 Abbreviations	英文全称 Grammatical terms in English	语法术语 Grammatical terms in Chinese	拼音 Grammatical terms in *pinyin*
S	Subject	主语	zhǔyǔ
P	Predicate	谓语	wèiyǔ
O	Object	宾语	bīnyǔ
Attr	Attribute	定语	dìngyǔ
A	Adverbial	状语	zhuàngyǔ
Comp	Complement	补语	bǔyǔ
NP	Noun Phrase	名词短语	míngcí duǎnyǔ
VP	Verbal Phrase	动词短语	dòngcí duǎnyǔ
PP	Prepositional Phrase	介词短语	jiècí duǎnyǔ
V O	Verb-object Phrase	动宾短语	dòng-bīn duǎnyǔ
	Declarative Sentence	陈述句	chénshùjù
	Interrogative Sentence	疑问句	yíwènjù
	Affirmative Sentence	肯定句	kěndìngjù
	Negative Sentence	否定句	fǒudìngjù
	General Interrogative Sentence	一般疑问句	yìbān yíwènjù
	Special Interrogative Sentence	特殊疑问句	tèshū yíwènjù
	Yes-or-no Question	是非疑问句	shìfēi yíwènjù
	Affirmative and Negative Question	正反疑问句	zhèngfǎn yíwènjù

主要人物介绍
Introduction of the main characters

Kǎ'ěr
卡尔
Karl Hofmann

Kāng Àilì
康爱丽
Alice Clement

Lǐ Míngming
李明明
Li Mingming

Zhāng Yuǎn
张远
Zhang Yuan

卡　尔——男，德国人，欧盟经理人；

康爱丽——女，法国人，欧盟经理人；

李明明——女，中国人，对外经济贸易大学国贸专业本科三年级学生；

张　远——男，中国人，对外经济贸易大学MBA二年级学生。

　　康爱丽、卡尔都是来北京接受汉语培训的欧盟经理人，李明明和张远是他们在对外经济贸易大学认识的朋友。

Ka'er—Karl Hofmann, male, a German manager from the European Union;

Kang Aili—Alice Clement, female, a French manager from the European Union;

Li Mingming—female, a Chinese junior majoring in International Trade at University of International Business and Economics;

Zhang Yuan—male, a Chinese MBA sophomore at University of International Business and Economics.

　　Both Kang Aili (Alice) and Ka'er (Karl) are managers from the European Union who came to Beijing for the training of Chinese language. Li Mingming and Zhang Yuan are their friends at University of International Business and Economics.

第六单元
UNIT **6**
超市和机场
Supermarket and airport

学校附近有超市吗
Is there a supermarket near the school

课文 Text	题目 Title	注释 Notes
一	学校附近有超市吗 Is there a supermarket near the school	1. "有"字句（2） The "有"-sentence (2) 2. 动词"在" The verb "在" 3. "南边"、"北边"及方位词介绍 "南边","北边" and an introduction of locality nouns 4. 副词"更" The adverb "更" 5. 疑问代词"怎么"（复习） The interrogative pronoun "怎么" (Review) 6. 指路的表示法 How to ask for directions 7. 副词"就" The adverb "就"
二	收银台在哪儿 Where is the cashier	1. 介词"在"（复习） The preposition "在" (Review) 2. 副词"不用" The adverb "不用" 3. 方位词"下"及单纯方位词 The locality noun "下" and simple locality nouns 4. 动态助词"着" The aspect particle "着" 5. 人称代词"自己" The personal pronoun "自己" 6. 方位词"旁边"及合成方位词 The locality noun "旁边" and compound locality nouns

三	机场离这儿远吗 Is the airport far away from here	1. 动词"离" The verb "离" 2. 副词"大概" The adverb "大概" 3. 副词"多" The adverb "多" 4. 假设复句:"(如果 / 要是)……的话,……就……" The hypothetical complex sentence: "(如果 / 要是)……的话,……就……" 5. 副词"差不多" The adverb "差不多" 6. 疑问代词短语作定语 The interrogative pronoun phrase acts as an attribute 7. 副词"已经" The adverb "已经" 8. 表示新情况的语气助词"了₂" The modal particle "了₂" used to indicate a new situation 9. "没问题" 10. 能愿动词"得(děi)" The optative verb "得(děi)" 11. 语气助词"呢" The modal particle "呢" 12. 动态助词"了₁" The aspect particle "了₁"

Xuéxiào Fùjìn Yǒu Chāoshì ma
学校附近有超市吗
Is there a supermarket near the school

> Kǎ'ěr hé Lǐ Míngming zài xuéxiào ménkǒu.
> 卡尔和李明明在学校门口。
> Karl and Li Mingming are standing at the gate of the school.

Kǎ'ěr: Xuéxiào fùjìn yǒu chāoshì ma?

● 卡尔： 学校附近有超市吗？

Karl: Is there a supermarket near the school?

Lǐ Míngming: Yǒu. Xuéxiào fùjìn yǒu liǎng jiā chāoshì, Jiālèfú hé Wò'ěrmǎ.

○ 李明明： 有。学校附近有两家超市，家乐福和沃尔玛。

Li Mingming: Yes, there are two supermarkets near the school: Carrefour and Walmart.

Kǎ'ěr: Zài nǎr?

● 卡尔： 在哪儿？

Karl: Where are they?

Lǐ Míngming: Jiālèfú zài xuéxiào de nánbian, Wò'ěrmǎ zài xuéxiào de běibian.

○ 李明明： 家乐福在学校的南边，沃尔玛在学校的北边。

Li Mingming: Carrefour lies to the south of the school, and Walmart the north.

Kǎ'ěr: Nǎ jiā gèng jìn?
● 卡尔: 哪家更近？
Karl: Which one is nearer?

Lǐ Míngming: Jiālèfú.
○ 李明明: 家乐福。
Li Mingming: Carrefour.

Kǎ'ěr: Zěnme zǒu?
● 卡尔: 怎么走？
Karl: How can I get there?

Lǐ Míngming: Guò mǎlù, yìzhí wǎng qián zǒu, dào dì yī ge lùkǒu wǎng zuǒ guǎi,
○ 李明明: 过马路，一直往前走，到第一个路口往左拐，
jiù dào le.
就到了。
Li Mingming: Cross the street, go straight ahead and turn left at the first crossing, and then you will see it.

Kǎ'ěr: Xièxie!
● 卡尔: 谢谢！
Karl: Thanks!

生词 Shēngcí New Words

1. 附近	fùjìn	N	near, nearby
2. 超市	chāoshì	N	supermarket
3. 和	hé	Conj	and
4. 在	zài	V	to exist, to be, to lie
5. 南边	nánbian	N	south
边	bian	Suf	*suffix of location words*
6. 北边	běibian	N	north
7. 更	gèng	Adv	more, even more
8. 近	jìn	Adj	near
9. 过	guò	V	to cross

10. 马路	mǎlù	N	street, road
11. 一直	yìzhí	Adv	straight
12. 往	wǎng	Prep	to, towards
13. 前	qián	N	front
14. 到	dào	V	to arrive
15. 第	dì	Suf	*used before integers to indicate order, such as lst, 10th*
16. 路口	lùkǒu	N	crossing, intersection
17. 左	zuǒ	N	left
18. 拐	guǎi	V	to turn

专有名词 Zhuānyǒu míngcí **Proper Nouns**

| 1. 家乐福 | Jiālèfú | Carrefour |
| 2. 沃尔玛 | Wò'ěrmǎ | Walmart |

注释 Zhùshì **Notes**

1 **学校附近有超市吗？** **Is there a supermarket near the school?**

"有"字句。我们在第一单元课文一中学过"有"字句表示"拥有"的用法。这里是另外一种用法，表示"某地存在某人或某事"，和英文里的"there be…"用法类似。主语是表示处所的名词短语，宾语多带数量词，有时数量词也可省略。基本结构：处所词语 + "有" + 数量词 + 名词。例如：

In Text 1, Unit 1, we have learned that the "有"-sentence indicates "have". This is another usage, that is, "有" indicates there is somebody or something at some place. It is similar to "there be…" in English. The subject can be a noun phrase indicating place. Its object often takes a quantifier；sometimes the quantifier can be omitted. The basic pattern is: words of place + "有" + quantifier + noun. For example,

S	P	
PW	V（有）	Q＋NP（O）
学校附近	有	（一家）超市。

肯定句	Affirmative sentence	学校附近有（一家）超市。
否定句	Negative sentence	学校附近没有超市。
疑问句	Interrogative sentence	学校附近有超市吗？

在表示存在的"有"字句中，对宾语和主语提问要用不同的疑问代词。例如：

If a "有"-sentence is used to indicate the existence of somebody or something, different pronouns are used to question the object and the subject. For example,

① 学校附近有什么？（提问宾语　To ask about the object.）

② 哪儿有超市？／超市在哪儿？

（提问表示处所的主语　To ask about the subject indicating place.）

注意："有"后的宾语是不定指的。宾语表示的人或事物不是主语表示的处所范围里的唯一存在，还有别的东西。例如：

Note: The object after "有" is non-specific, and the person or thing it denotes is not the only one at the place the subject indicates. For example,

③ 学校对面（duìmiàn, opposite）有一家超市。（不定指　unspecific）（√）

④ 学校对面有这家超市。（定指　specific）（×）

2 家乐福在学校的南边，沃尔玛在学校的北边。

Carrefour lies to the south of the school, and Walmart the north.

"在"，动词，表示人或事物存在的处所、位置，一般要带宾语。基本结构：名词／名词短语＋"在"＋方位词。例如：

The verb "在" indicates the place or position of somebody or something. It is generally followed by an object. Its basic pattern is: noun / noun phrase ＋ "在" ＋ locality noun. For example,

S	P	
N／NP	V（在）	PW（O）
家乐福	在	学校的南边。
沃尔玛		学校的北边。

肯定句 Affirmative sentence	家乐福在学校的南边。
否定句 Negative sentence	家乐福不在学校的南边。
一般疑问句 General interrogative sentence	家乐福在学校的南边吗？
特殊疑问句 Special interrogative sentence	家乐福在哪儿？ （提问宾语　To ask about the object.） 哪儿有家乐福？ （提问表示处所的主语　To ask about the location the subject indicates.）

3　家乐福在学校的南边，沃尔玛在学校的北边。

Carrefour lies to the south of the school, and Walmart the north.

"南边"、"北边"，方位词。

"南边" and "北边" are locality nouns.

（1）汉语中的单纯方位词"东、西、南、北、上、下、前、后、左、右、中、里、内、外、旁"一般不单用，常和"边、面"等组成合成方位词。请看下表：

The simple locality nouns in Chinese, such as "东"，"西"，"南"，"北"，"上"，"下"，"前"，"后"，"左"，"右"，"中"，"里"，"内"，"外"，"旁", are usually not used by themselves, but often used together with "边" or "面" to form compound locality nouns. Please read the following form:

单纯方位词 Simple location words	边	面（miàn）
东（dōng, east）	东边	东面
西（xī, west）	西边	西面
南	南边	南面
北	北边	北面
上（shàng, up）	上边	上面
下（xià, down）	下边	下面
左	左边	左面
右（yòu, right）	右边	右面
前	前边	前面
后（hòu, back）	后边	后面

（续表）

单纯方位词 Simple location words	边	面（miàn）
里（lǐ, inside）	里边	里面
外（wài, outside）	外边	外面
旁（páng, beside）	旁边	/

注意："中（zhōng, middle）"一般与"间（jiān, between, among）"构成"中间"。

Note: "中（zhōng, middle)" is generally used with "间 (jiān, between, among)" to form "中间".

（2）单纯方位词也可以和一般的表示处所的名词组合。例如：

A simple locality noun can also be used together with a common noun of place. For example,

① 书在桌子上。

② 他在公寓里。

（3）合成方位词可以在"有"字句中充当主语。例如：

A compound locality noun can serve as the subject in a "有"-sentences. For example,

③ 南边有一家超市。

④ 外面有很多人。

（4）方位词常和"在"等介词组成"介词＋名词＋方位词"短语，"在"有时可省略。例如，"在学校南边有一家超市"和"学校南边有一家超市"意思相同。但如果省略方位词，变成"学校有一家超市"，那么意思就改变了。

Locality nouns are often used together with some prepositions, like "在", to form the structure of "preposition + noun + locality noun". "在" is omitted sometimes. For example, "在学校南边有一家超市" is equivalent in meaning to "学校南边有一家超市", but "学校有一家超市" is different in meaning if the locality noun is omitted.

4 **哪家更近？ Which one is nearer?**

"更"，副词，表示程度加深。常用在动词短语或形容词的前面，作状语。"更"用作比较，句中常有对比的两个方面，而且应该一方比另一方的程度更深。没有比较时，不能用"更"。例如：

The adverb "更" indicates the degree is stronger. It is often used as an adverbial before a verb phrase or an adjective. "更" is used to compare two things and one is stronger in degree than the other. "更" is not used if no comparison is made. For example,

① 他说得不好，我说得更不好。

② 这件白的很好看，不过，我更喜欢（xǐhuan, to like）那件蓝的。

③ 张老师和王老师，你更喜欢哪一个？

5 怎么走？ **How can I get there?**

"怎么"，疑问代词。"怎么＋动词"可以用来询问动作的方式。我们在第一册第五单元课文二中学过。例如：

"怎么" is an interrogative pronoun. "怎么＋ V" can be used to ask how to do something, which was learned in Text 2, Unit 5 of Book 1. For example,

S	P	
	怎么（Qpr）	V
电脑		开（kāi, to turn on）
这个字（zì, character）	怎么	写？
去图书馆（túshūguǎn, library）		走？

6 一直往前走，到第一个路口往左拐。 **Go straight ahead and turn left at the first crossing.**

指路用语。"一直"，副词，这里表示顺着一个方向不变。"往"，介词，表示动作的方向。后面要带表示方向的方位词，作动词的状语。"到"后是表示处所、方位的词语。例如：

The structure is often used to show directions. The adverb "一直" here means going straight towards a direction. The preposition "往" is followed by a locality noun. It indicates the direction of an action and serves as the adverbial of a verb. "到" is followed by words indicating place or direction. For example,

① 一直往前走，到第一个路口往右拐。

② 一直往西走，到第二个路口往左拐。

③ 一直往南走，到第三个红绿灯（hónglǜdēng, traffic light）往东拐。

7 到第一个路口往左拐，就到了。 **Turn left at the first crossing, and then you will see it.**

"就"，副词，这里表示它后面的动作紧接着前面的事情或动作发生。后面常加助词"了"。例如：

The adverb "就" indicates an action happens right after the preceding one. It is often followed by the particle "了". For example,

① 他说完就走了。

② 我送他到车站（chēzhàn, stop）后，就回学校了。

③ 你打开窗户就能看见。

Shōuyíntái Zài Nǎr

收银台在哪儿

Where is the cashier

Kǎ'ěr zài chāoshì.

卡尔在超市。

Karl is at the supermarket.

Kǎ'ěr: Qǐngwèn, zhèr yǒu Fǎguó hóngjiǔ ma?

● 卡尔: 请问，这儿有法国红酒吗？

Karl: Excuse me, is there French red wine?

Shòuhuòyuán: Yǒu, jiù zài qiánbian. Wǎng yòu guǎi, zài yòubian de huòjià shang.

○ 售货员: 有，就在前边。往右拐，在右边的货架上。

Shop assistant: Yes, just go ahead. Turn right, you will find it on the shelf on the right.

Kǎ'ěr: Xièxie!

● 卡尔: 谢谢！

Karl: Thanks!

Shòuhuòyuán: Xiānsheng, wǒmen zuìjìn xīn tuīchū yì kuǎn guóchǎn hóngjiǔ,
○ 售货员： 先生，我们最近新推出一款国产红酒，
wù měi jià lián, nín chángchang!
物美价廉，您尝尝！
Shop assistant: Sir, we are promoting a kind of Chinese red wine these days. It's of excellent quality and reasonable price. Please have a try!

Kǎ'ěr: Xièxie! Búyòng le!
● 卡尔： 谢谢！不用了！
Karl: No, thank you!

Shòuhuòyuán: Xiānsheng, jiǔ yào zài zhèr jiāo qián, bú zài lóu xià jiāo.
○ 售货员： 先生，酒要在这儿交钱，不在楼下交。
Shop assistant: Sir, please pay for the wine here, not downstairs.

Kǎ'ěr: Hǎo de, zhīdao le.
● 卡尔： 好的，知道了。
Karl: OK. I got it.

Shòuhuòyuán: Yǒu nín yào de páizi ma?
○ 售货员： 有您要的牌子吗？
Shop assistant: Is there the brand you want?

Kǎ'ěr: Wǒ zhèng zhǎozhe ne.
● 卡尔： 我正找着呢。
Karl: I am looking for it.

Shòuhuòyuán: Yào wǒ bāngmáng ma?
○ 售货员： 要我帮忙吗？
Shop assistant: Can I help you?

Kǎ'ěr: Wǒ zìjǐ zhǎo ba.
● 卡尔： 我自己找吧。
Karl: I can find it by myself.

Shòuhuòyuán: Hǎo de, nín yǒu shìr jiào wǒ.
○ 售货员： 好的，您有事儿叫我。
Shop assistant: OK. Please call me if you need anything.

Kǎ'ěr: Děng yíxià! Qǐngwèn, shōuyíntái zài nǎr?
● 卡尔： 等一下！请问，收银台在哪儿？
Karl: Wait a minute! Excuse me, where is the cashier?

Shòuhuòyuán: Zài nàbiān. Kàn, diàntī pángbiān.

○ 售货员： 在那边。看，电梯旁边。

Shop assistant: Over there. Look, next to the elevator.

Kǎ'ěr: Xièxie!

● 卡尔： 谢谢！

Karl: Thanks!

生词　Shēngcí　New Words

1. 收银台	shōuyíntái	N	checkout counter, cashier
2. 这儿	zhèr	Pr	here
3. 红酒	hóngjiǔ	N	red wine
4. 右	yòu	N	right
5. 货架	huòjià	N	shelf
6. 上	shang	N	above, over, on top of, on the surface of
7. 推出	tuīchū	V	to promote
8. 款	kuǎn	M	(a measure word) kind, style
9. 国产	guóchǎn	Adj	made in one's own country
10. 物美价廉	wù měi jià lián		of excellent quality and reasonable price
11. 不用	búyòng	Adv	not need
12. 酒	jiǔ	N	wine
13. 交	jiāo	V	to pay
14. 楼	lóu	N	floor, storey
15. 下	xià	N	below, down, underneath
16. 牌子	páizi	N	brand
17. 正	zhèng	Adv	*indicating an action or state is going on*
18. 着	zhe	AP	*an aspect particle*
19. 帮忙	bāng máng	V//O	to help, to do (sb.) a favour
20. 自己	zìjǐ	Pr	oneself

21. 那边	nàbiān	Pr	there
22. 电梯	diàntī	N	elevator
23. 旁边	pángbiān	N	side, adjacent place

注释　Zhùshì　**Notes**

1　**在右边的货架上。**　**You will find it on the shelf on the right.**

"在"，介词，我们在第二单元课文三中学过这种用法。这里介词"在"和时间、处所、方位等词语组成介宾短语，表示处所和时间。"在"有时可省略，后面的词语不能省略。例如：

We have learned how the preposition "在" is used this way in Text 3, Unit 2. In this case, the preposition "在" is used with a word denoting time, place or locality to form a prepositional phrase. It indicates the place or time. "在" can be omitted sometimes. However, the words after "在" cannot be omitted. For example,

① A：卡尔在哪儿？

　　B：在教室里。／教室里。

② A：你的书呢？

　　B：在桌子上。／桌子上。

表示处所　To indicate place：

在家里（中）　　在床上／下　　在卡尔的衣服上　　在左边的椅子上

在收银台上　　　在窗前　　　　在教室的门后

表示时间　To indicate time：

在考试（kǎoshì, to test）前（之前、以前）

在回家后（之后、以后）

2　**谢谢！不用了！**　**No, thank you!**

"不用"，副词，表示事实上没有必要。"不用了"，意思是"不要了"，表示拒绝。例如：

The adverb "不用" indicates there is no need actually. "不用了" means it is unnecessary and indicating the speaker's refusal. For example,

① 售货员：我帮你找吧。

　　顾客（gùkè, customer）：不用了。

②A：先生，您试试这件衣服吧。

B：谢谢，不用了。

③老板，给您钱，不用找了。

3 不在楼下交。 **Not downstairs.**

"下"，方位名词。名词或名词短语后直接加单音节方位词"上、下、里、外、前、后"等，组成表示处所的短语。例如：

"下" is a locality noun. A noun or noun phrase and a monosyllable locality noun, such as "上", "下", "里", "外", "前" or "后", form a phrase indicating place. For example,

床上／床下　　楼上／楼下／楼里／楼外　　门前／门后　　桌旁／桌上／桌下
右边的货架上　　学校的超市里　　我的手上　　他的脚边

注意：　Note：

（1）用在名词后的"上、里"要读轻声。

"上" and "里" used after a noun is pronounced in the neutral tone.

（2）在汉语中，用普通名词表示处所时，后面往往要加上方位词。但是国名和地名的后面不能再用方位词"里"。例如：

In Chinese, when a common noun is used to indicate place, it is often followed by a locality noun. However, the locality noun "里" cannot be used after the name of a country or a place. For example,

①教室里在开会。（√）

教室在开会。（×）

②他们在楼下等你。（√）

他们在楼等你。（×）

③我们在北京学汉语。（√）

我们在北京里学汉语。（×）

4 我正找着呢。 **I am looking for it.**

"着"，动态助词，用在动词后面，表示动作正在进行。动词前可以有副词"正、在、正在"，句末常有表示进行的助词"呢"。例如：

The aspect particle "着" is used after a verb to indicate an action is going on. An adverb like "正", "在" or "正在" can be used before the verb. The particle "呢" is often used at the end of a sentence to indicate something is going on. For example,

①我们正开着会。

②卡尔在上着课呢。

③康爱丽和她的朋友们唱着、跳着。

注意： **Note:**

（1）动词后面用 "着" 以后，只能带宾语，不能带其他动态助词或补语。

When a verb is followed by "着", it can only take an object, not another aspect particle or complement.

（2）不是所有的动词后面都能带 "着"，下面是不能带 "着" 的几种情况：

Not all the verbs can be followed by "着". In the following cases, "着" is not used.

A. 本身不能表示持续行为的动词，如 "是、在、进、去、来、出、到、见、懂、死、忘、姓、祝、完、没有、明白、告诉、感到、感觉、觉得、等于、开始、结束、爱好" 等。

Verbs that do not indicate the continuation of an action, for example, "是"，"在"，"进"，"去"，"来"，"出"，"到"，"见"，"懂"，"死"，"忘"，"姓"，"祝"，"完"，"没有"，"明白"，"告诉"，"感到"，"感觉"，"觉得"，"等于"，"开始"，"结束"，"爱好"，etc.

B. 本身有持续意思的动词，如 "知道、认识、同意、需要" 等。

Verbs that indicate the continuation of an action themselves, for example, "知道"，"认识"，"同意"，"需要"，etc.

C. 前边有能愿动词的时候。例如：

When verbs preceded by optative verbs. For example,

④ 他能上着课。（×）

⑤ 我可以写着邮件。（×）

⑥ 明明想买着苹果。（×）

5 **我自己找吧。** **I can find it by myself.**

"自己"，人称代词，复指句中已经出现的人，和 "别人（biéren, other people）" 相对。基本用法：

The personal pronoun "自己" refers to the person that has already been there in the sentence. Its antonym is "别人". Basic usage：

（1）与其他人称代词或名词结合起来作主语、宾语，强调某人本人或事物本身。例如：

It can be used as a subject or an object together with another personal pronoun or noun. It emphasizes the person him / herself or the thing itself. For example,

① 他自己去上海了。

② 这是王老师自己的事儿。

③ 电脑自己关机了。

（2）单用，称代在主语位置上的人称代词或名词，作宾语、定语等。例如：

It is used on its own to refer to the personal pronoun or noun which is the subject of the sentence. It is used as an object or an attribute, etc. For example,

④ 小张给自己买了一件衣服。

⑤ 卡尔拿自己的钱帮助孩子们。

⑥ 他不告诉我们，自己去医院（yīyuàn, hospital）了。

⑦ 自己的事情自己做。

（3）单用，修饰动词、形容词，作状语。例如：

It is used on its own to modify a verb or an adjective serving as an adverbial. For example,

⑧ 想喝咖啡，自己买。

⑨ 明明常自己做饭吃。

⑩ 这种感冒（gǎnmào, cold）不用吃药，过一个星期就会自己好的。

⑪ 灯自己亮了。

6 **看，电梯旁边。** Look, next to the elevator.

"旁边"，合成方位词，可以放在名词或名词短语的后面，组成表示处所的短语。

"旁边" is a compound locality noun. It is placed after a noun or noun phrase to form a phrase of place.

名词用在带"边、头、面"的合成方位词的前面时，中间一般不用"的"，有时加"的"，表示意义的重点在合成方位词上。例如：

If the noun is used before a compound locality noun like "边", "头", or "面", "的" is generally not used in between. Sometimes, "的" is used to indicate that the compound locality noun is the focus of meaning. For example,

货架左边 / 货架的左边　　　椅子上边 / 椅子的上边

公寓里面 / 公寓的里面　　　超市里头 / 超市的里头

学校外边 / 学校的外边

Jīchǎng Lí Zhèr Yuǎn ma

机场离这儿远吗

Is the airport far away from here

Kāng Àilì zuò chūzūchē qù fēijīchǎng.

康爱丽坐出租车去飞机场。

Alice takes a taxi to the airport.

Sījī: Nín hǎo! Nín qù nǎr?

● 司机：   您好！您去哪儿？

Taxi driver: Good morning! Where are you going?

Kāng Àilì: Wǒ qù jīchǎng. Jīchǎng lí zhèr yuǎn ma?

○ 康爱丽：   我去机场。机场离这儿远吗？

Alice: The airport. Is the airport far away from here?

Sījī: Tǐng yuǎn de.

● 司机：   挺远的。

Taxi driver: Pretty far.

Kāng Àilì: Dàgài duō cháng shíjiān?

○ 康爱丽：   大概多长时间？

Alice: How long will it probably take?

司机: Bù dǔchē dehuà, chàbuduō sìshí fēnzhōng.

● 司机: 不堵车的话，差不多 40 分钟。

Taxi driver: About 40 minutes if there is no traffic jam.

Kāng Àilì: Qǐng kuài yìdiǎnr, wǒ yǒu jí shìr.

○ 康爱丽: 请快一点儿，我有急事儿。

Alice: A little faster, please. I'm in a hurry.

Sījī: Hǎo de. Nín jǐ diǎn de fēijī?

● 司机: 好的。您几点的飞机？

Taxi driver: OK. What time does your plane take off?

Kāng Àilì: Wǒ qù jiē yí wèi péngyou, tā shì shíyī diǎn de fēijī.

○ 康爱丽: 我去接一位朋友，他是 11 点的飞机。

Alice: I'm picking up a friend, whose plane is going to take off at 11 o'clock.

Sījī: Láidejí. Jǐ hào hángzhànlóu?

● 司机: 来得及。几号航站楼？

Taxi driver: We still have enough time. Which terminal?

Kāng Àilì: Sān hào. Xiànzài yǐjīng shí diǎn le, wǒ bù néng chídào!

○ 康爱丽: 3 号。现在已经 10 点了，我不能迟到！

Alice: Terminal 3. It's already 10 o'clock now. I mustn't be late.

Sījī: Méi wèntí! Zǒu jīchǎng gāosù hěn kuài. Nín de péngyou hái děi qǔ

● 司机: 没问题！走机场高速很快。您的朋友还得取

xíngli ne.

行李呢。

Taxi driver: No problem! It will be pretty fast if we take the airport expressway. In addition, your friend will have to get his luggage.

Kāng Àilì: Xièxie!

○ 康爱丽: 谢谢！

Alice: Thank you!

Zài jīchǎng.

在机场。

In the airport.

Kāng Àilì: Jiù tíng zhèr ba. Duōshao qián?

○ 康爱丽: 就停这儿吧。多少钱？

Alice: You can just stop here. How much is it?

Sījī: Sìshíbā.
● 司机：   48。
Taxi driver: 48.

Kāng Àilì: Gěi nín wǔshí, búyòng zhǎo le.
○ 康爱丽：   给您50，不用找了。
Alice: Here is 50, and you can keep the change.

Sījī: Xièxie. Gěi nín fāpiào. Bié wàngle nín de dōngxi.
● 司机：   谢谢。给您发票。别忘了您的东西。
Taxi driver: Thank you. Here is the receipt. Don't forget to take your personal belongings with you.

Kāng Àilì: Hǎo de. Xièxie!
○ 康爱丽：   好的。谢谢！
Alice: OK, thank you.

Sījī: Bú kèqi. Zàijiàn!
● 司机：   不客气。再见！
Taxi driver: You are welcome. Goodbye!

Kāng Àilì: Zàijiàn!
○ 康爱丽：   再见！
Alice: Goodbye!

生词 Shēngcí New Words

1. 机场	jīchǎng	N	airport
2. 离	lí	V	to be away from
3. 远	yuǎn	Adj	far
4. 司机	sījī	N	driver
5. 大概	dàgài	Adv	probably
6. 多	duō	Adv	how
7. 长	cháng	Adj	long
8. 时间	shíjiān	N	time
9. 堵车	dǔ chē	V//O	to have a traffic jam

10. 的话	dehuà	Pt	*a particle indicating supposition*
11. 差不多	chàbuduō	Adv	almost
12. 分钟	fēnzhōng	N	minute
13. 急	jí	Adj	hurried
14. 飞机	fēijī	N	plane, airplane
15. 接	jiē	V	to meet, to pick up
16. 航站楼	hángzhànlóu	N	terminal
17. 已经	yǐjīng	Adv	already
18. 问题	wèntí	N	problem
19. 高速	gāosù	Adj	high speed
20. 得	děi	OpV	have to, need
21. 取	qǔ	V	to get, to take
22. 行李	xíngli	N	luggage
23. 停	tíng	V	to stop
24. 发票	fāpiào	N	receipt
25. 忘	wàng	V	to forget
26. 东西	dōngxi	N	thing

注释 Zhùshì Notes

1 机场离这儿远吗? Is the airport far away from here?

"离",动词,表示距离。常用来表示两个地点之间的远近,后面常用形容词"远"和"近"。基本结构:Place 1 + "离" + Place 2 + "远(近)"。例如:

"离", a verb, indicates distance. It is often used to denote the distance between two places, and it is often followed by the adjective "远" or "近". The basic structure is: Place 1 + "离" + Place 2 + "远 (近)". For example,

S		A		Adj
Place 1	V（离）	Place 2		
学校	离	超市		远吗？

肯定句	Affirmative sentence	学校离超市很远/近。
否定句	Negative sentence	学校离超市不远。
疑问句	Interrogative sentence	学校离超市远吗？

2 大概多长时间？ How long will it probably take?

"大概"，副词，表示对时间、数量的不精确估计，作状语。后面可以带时间词、数量词。可放在句首，也可在句中。例如：

"大概" is an adverb to denote an approximate estimation of time or amount. It can be used as an adverbial at the beginning or middle of a sentence and followed by words denoting time or amount. For example,

① 她大概有 30 岁。

② A：你睡了多长时间？

　B：大概两个小时。

③ 卡尔大概明年 5 月回国（huí guó, to return to one's country）。

3 大概多长时间？ How long will it probably take?

"多"，副词，用在疑问句中询问数量或程度，后面根据询问的内容带相应的形容词，如 "长、久、大、高" 等，组成 "多 + Adj" 的结构。

"多", an adverb, is used in an interrogative sentence to inquire amount or degree. A corresponding adjective is put after it, such as "长", "久", "大", or "高" to form the structure "多 + Adj".

（1）"多 + 远"，询问距离。例如：

"多 + 远" can be used to inquire distance. For example,

　　① 学校离机场多远？

　　② 你的宿舍离教室多远？

（2）"多 + 久" 或 "多 + 长 + 时间"，询问时间长短。例如：

"多 + 久" or "多 + 长 + 时间" can be used to inquire length of time. For example,

　　③ 走路去学校要多长时间？

　　④ 今天下午的研讨会要多久？

（3）"多＋大"，询问事物大小。例如：

"多＋大" can be used to inquire the size of something. For example,

⑤ 这间教室多大？

⑥ 这家公司多大？

（4）"多＋大（＋年纪）"，询问年龄。例如：

"多＋大 (+age)" can be used to inquire somebody's age. For example,

⑦ A：卡尔多大了？

B：卡尔 30（岁）。

⑧ A：你（今年）多大年纪（niánjì, age）？

B：我（今年）29（岁）。

4 不堵车的话，差不多40分钟。About 40 minutes if there is no traffic jam.

假设复句。前一分句提出一个假设的情况，后一分句表示由假设情况产生的结果或推论。"的话"，助词，用在表示假设关系的分句末尾。假设分句的句首可以有"如果（rúguǒ, if）、要是（yàoshi, if）"等表示假设的连词和"的话"呼应；后一分句中常用副词"就"。这句话完整的表达应该是："如果／要是不堵车的话，差不多 40 分钟就到了"。基本结构："（如果／要是）……的话，……就……"。例如：

In a hypothetical complex sentence, the first clause puts forward a hypothetical situation, while the second indicates the hypothesized result or conclusion. "的话" is a particle used at the end of a hypothetical clause, which is preceded by a suppositive conjunction, like "如果 (rúguǒ, if)" or "要是 (yàoshi, if)". In the second clause, the adverb "就" is frequently used. The complete sentence is "如果／要是不堵车的话，差不多40分钟就到了". The basic structure is: "（如果／要是）……的话，……就……". For example,

clause 1			clause 2		
Conj（如果／要是）	Sub-sentence / VP	Pt（的话）	S		P
如果	明天天气好		我们		一起去公园。
要是	便宜一点儿	的话，	我	就	买。
	有时间		我		去上海。

5 差不多40分钟。About 40 minutes.

"差不多"，副词，表示对数量的估计，跟"大概"意思相同。例如：

"差不多" is an adverb indicating an estimation of amount. It is equivalent to "大概". For example,

S	P	
	Adv（差不多）	Q + N
从学校走路到超市	差不多	10分钟。
从学校坐出租车到飞机场		40块钱。

6 您几点的飞机？   What time does your plane take off?

"几点"，询问时间的疑问代词短语，可作定语，在它和名词性词语中间要加"的"。类似的疑问代词短语作定语的还有"几号、多大、多少钱、多长时间"等。例如：

"几点" is an interrogative pronoun phrase used to inquire time. It can be used as an attribute. "的" is used between "几点" and the nominal phrase. Other similar interrogative pronoun phrases used as an attribute include "几号", "多大", "多少钱", and "多长时间", etc. For example,

① 你们几点的课？

② 你要买几号的票（piào, ticket）？

③ 你想买多少钱的衣服？

④ 你要做多长时间的作业？

⑤ 这是多大的公司？

7 现在已经10点了。   It's already 10 o'clock now.

"已经"，副词，表时间。可作状语，放在形容词或动词前，表示过去某时间内发生的动作或状态。这里是用在表示时间的名词谓语句中，"已经"在名词性谓语前作状语。

"已经" is an adverb to indicate time. It can be used as an adverbial before an adjective or a verb to indicate an action taken place or a state going on in a certain time. Here "已经" is used in a nominal predicate sentence indicating time and is used as an adverbial before the nominal predicate.

8 现在已经10点了。   It's already 10 o'clock now.

"了"，语气助词，放在句末，表示情况变化或出现了新情况，有成句的作用，同时还可以表示确定的语气，在汉语语法里又叫"了₂"。这时动词如果有宾语，"了"要放在宾语的后面。例如：

The particle "了" is used at the end of a sentence to indicate a change or a new situation in an affirmative tone. It is also known as "了₂" in Chinese grammar. If a verb is followed by an object, "了" is used after the object. For example,

S	P	
他的病（bìng, illness）	好	
	下课	了。
天气	冷	
卡尔	30岁	

9 没问题！ No problem!

"没问题"，用来回答别人的疑问或请求，表示可以做到，也可以说"行、好、好的"。

It is used to answer others' questions or request, indicating the speaker can do it. "行", "好" or "好的" can also be used.

10 您的朋友还得取行李呢。In addition, your friend will have to get his luggage.

"得（děi）"，能愿动词，表示情理或事实上的需要。"得"比"应该"的语气更肯定、更口语化。否定形式是"不用、不必"，不说"不得"。例如：

"得", an optative verb, indicates a need based on common sense or reality. It is more affirmative and colloquial than "应该". Its negative form is "不用" or "不必", but not "不得". For example,

S	P	
	OpV（得）	VP / Adj
我		先吃饭。
我	得	早点儿睡觉。
你		便宜点儿。
你		努力学习。

肯定句　Affirmative sentence	否定句　Negative sentence
他明天得工作。	他明天不用/不必工作。
你今天晚上得早点儿睡觉。	你今天晚上不用/不必早睡觉。
我得回家。	我不用/不必回家。

11 您的朋友还得取行李呢。   **In addition, your friend will have to get his luggage.**

"呢"，语气助词，不表示疑问，而是用在句尾表示确认事实，使对方相信。

The modal particle "呢" is used at the end of a sentence to confirm a fact and convince the listener. It is not used for interrogation.

12 别忘了您的东西。**Don't forget to take your personal belongings with you.**

"了"，动态助词，放在动词后，表示动作的完成或实现。在汉语语法里也叫"了₁"。例如：

"了" is an aspect particle used after a verb to indicate the completion or realization of an action. It is also known as "$了_1$" in Chinese grammar. For example,

S	P		
	V	Pt（了）	O
他	买		三本书。
我们	学	了	五课。
卡尔	发		一封邮件。
我们公司	有		很多新客户。

否定"了₁"时，在动词前加"没（有）"，动词后不带"了₁"。例如：

"$了_1$" is negated by using "没（有）" before a verb and "$了_1$" is not used after the verb. For example,

肯定句 Affirmative sentence	我昨天买了很多衣服。
否定句 Negative sentence	我昨天没（有）买衣服。
一般疑问句 General interrogative sentence	你昨天买衣服了吗？
特殊疑问句 Special interrogative sentence	你昨天买了什么？

注意：下面是不能使用"了₁"的情况：

Note: "$了_1$" is not used in the following cases:

（1）表示经常性行为的句子。例如：

In a sentence that indicates sb. does sth. on a regular basis. For example,

① 每天早上她都听了天气预报（yùbào, forecast）。（×）

（2）在能愿动词的后面。例如：

After an optative verb. For example,

　　②她能<u>了</u>去上课。（×）

（3）在表示心理活动的动词的后面。例如：

After a verb indicating mental activity. For example,

　　③他喜欢<u>了</u>音乐。（×）

（4）在否定句中。例如：

In a negative sentence. For example,

　　④他没去<u>了</u>机场。（×）

（5）在"……以前"的结构中。例如：

In the structure "……以前". For example,

　　⑤在来<u>了</u>北京以前，他在一家贸易公司当经理。（×）

（6）在"……时／的时候"中。例如：

In the structure "…… 时/的时候". For example,

　　⑥他去<u>了</u>超市的时候，碰到（pèngdào, to run into）了王老师。（×）

（7）在"是……的"句中。例如：

In the "是……的" sentence. For example,

　　⑦我是昨天去<u>了</u>超市的。（×）

（8）在动词作宾语的句子中。例如：

In a sentence using a verb as the object. For example,

　　⑧他打算（dǎsuàn, to plan）<u>了</u>去上海。（×）

练习　Liànxí　**Exercises**

一　跟读生词，注意发音和声调。
Read the new words after the teacher and pay attention to your pronunciation and tones.

二　跟读课文，注意语音语调。
Read the texts after the teacher and pay attention to your pronunciation and intonation.

三　学生分组，分角色朗读课文一、二、三。
Divide the students into groups and read Texts 1, 2 & 3 in roles.

四　学生分组，不看书，分角色表演课文一、二。
Divide the students into groups and play the roles in Texts 1 & 2 without referring to the book.

五　角色扮演。（提示：角色可以互换。）
Role playing. (Note: the roles can be exchanged.)

1. 问路：两个学生一组，一个人问路，一个人指路。用课文里学过的词语和句子完成一段对话。可以自己画出路线图来说明。

Asking the way: Two students work as a group. One asks the way, and the other shows the direction. Complete a dialogue with the words and sentence you learned in the texts. You can also draw a map to explain.

2. 坐出租车：两个或三个学生一组，一个人做司机，其他人当乘客，乘客决定去什么地方并向司机提出乘车要求。用课文里学过的词语和句子完成一段对话。

Taking the taxi: Two or three students work as a group. One acts as the driver, and the rest act as the passengers. The passengers decide where to go. and tell it to the driver. Complete a dialogue with the words and sentences they learned in the texts.

六　复述课文一和课文三。
Retell Texts 1 & 3.

七 替换练习。
Substitution drills.

① <u>学校附近</u> 有 <u>两家超市</u>。

学校对面	一家银行
超市旁边	很多饭馆（fànguǎn, restaurant）
公司北边	两所（suǒ, a measure word for schools）学校
图书馆前边	很多宿舍楼（sùshèlóu, dormitory）

② <u>家乐福</u> 怎么 <u>走</u>？

那个字	写
机票（jīpiào, air ticket）	买
中国菜（Zhōngguó cài, Chinese dishes）	做
电脑	用

③ 一直 往 <u>前</u> <u>走</u>，就到了。

东	开
西	骑（qí, to ride）
南	跑
北	走

④ <u>我</u> 正 <u>找</u> 着 呢。

看

学习

听

刷牙

他们　　　　发邮件

卡尔和爱丽　　说话

我们　　　　喝茶

老师　　　　讲课（jiǎng kè, to lecture）

同学们　　　做作业

⑤ <u>收银台</u> 在哪儿？

洗手间（xǐshǒujiān, restroom）

食堂

超市

取行李的地方

王老师的办公室（bàngōngshì, office）

你的电脑

你们的作业

⑥ <u>飞机场</u> 离 <u>这儿</u> <u>很远</u>。

我家	那儿	不远
飞机场	学校	不太远
书店（shūdiàn, bookstore）	银行	很近
超市	医院	有点儿远

⑦ <u>不堵车</u> 的话，<u>差不多40分钟</u>。

这件衣服你喜欢	我送你
星期天没有事儿	我跟（gēn, with, and）你去看电影
明天不下雨（xià yǔ, to rain）	我去你家玩儿
便宜	我想买

八 用下面的词语组成句子。
Make sentences with the following words and expressions.

① 南边　家乐福　学校　在　的

② 往　右　第一个　拐　路口　到

③ 就　前边　法国　在　红酒

④ 国产　我们　一款　推出　新　红酒

⑤ 吗　的　牌子　您　要　有

⑥ 吗　我　帮忙　要

⑦ 我　您　事儿　有　叫

⑧ 坐　机场　她　去　出租车

⑨ 点　几　您　飞机　的

⑩ 还　行李　取　得　您的朋友　呢

九 完成句子。

Complete the sentences following the examples.

① 家乐福在学校的<u>南边</u>。

经贸大学在中日友好医院（Zhōng-Rì Yǒuhǎo Yīyuàn, China-Japan Friendship

Hospital）的＿＿＿＿＿＿＿＿＿＿。

他家在银行的＿＿＿＿＿＿＿＿＿＿。

那家饭馆在学校西门（xīmén, west gate）的＿＿＿＿＿＿＿＿＿＿。

超市在商场（shāngchǎng, department store）的＿＿＿＿＿＿＿＿＿＿。

商场在邮局的＿＿＿＿＿＿＿＿＿＿。

② 哪家超市更<u>近</u>？

这两件衣服，哪件更＿＿＿＿＿＿＿＿？

这么多饭馆，哪家更＿＿＿＿＿＿＿＿？

飞机和火车，哪个更＿＿＿＿＿＿＿＿？

这两个学生谁更＿＿＿＿＿＿＿＿？

这两间（jiān, a measure word for rooms）教室，哪间更＿＿＿＿＿＿？

③ 飞机场离这儿挺<u>远</u>的。

今天的天气挺＿＿＿＿＿＿＿＿的。

他的身体（shēntǐ, body）挺＿＿＿＿＿＿＿＿的。

那里的风景挺＿＿＿＿＿＿＿＿的。

坐地铁（dìtiě, subway）去那儿挺＿＿＿＿＿＿＿＿的。

他的公寓挺＿＿＿＿＿＿＿＿的。

④ 您的朋友还得<u>取行李</u>呢。

我的身体不舒服（shūfu, feel well），我得＿＿＿＿＿＿＿。

我没有钱了，我得＿＿＿＿＿＿＿＿。

明天要考试，今天我得＿＿＿＿＿＿＿＿。

下雨了，出去（chūqu, to go out）的时候（shíhou, time）你得＿＿＿＿＿＿

＿＿＿＿＿＿。

他需要别人帮忙，我得＿＿＿＿＿＿＿＿＿＿。

十 用"多"对画线部分提问。

Raise questions about the underlined part with "多".

Example：他今年35岁。 ⟶ 他今年多大？

① 银行离学校两百多米。 ⟶

② 我哥哥（gēge, elder brother）1米75。 ⟶

③ 这五个苹果重（zhòng, weight）3斤。 ⟶

④ 他来中国两个多月了。 ⟶

⑤ 这个房间30平米（píngmǐ, square meter）。 ⟶

十一 判断下面的句子是否正确。

Decide whether the following sentences are true (√) or false (×).

① 明明没买了苹果。 （　　　　）

② 他想了回国。 （　　　　）

③ 每天早上她都洗了澡。 （　　　　）

④ 在来了中国以前，他住在法国。 （　　　　）

⑤ 明天你不得（děi）去上课。 （　　　　）

⑥ 他去超市的时候，看见了卡尔。 （　　　　）

⑦ 我是在上海认识他的。 （　　　　）

⑧ 我们打算去法国了。 （　　　　）

⑨ 别忘你的包。 （　　　　）

⑩ 你可以了下课。 （　　　　）

⑪ 明明想买着电脑。 （　　　　）

⑫ 卡尔去着上海。 （　　　　）

⑬ 教室在开会。 （　　　　）

⑭ 我们在中国里学汉语。 （　　　　）

十二 阅读理解。
Reading comprehension.

　　这是一张商店的平面图。从商店的南门进去，对面就是卖吃的的地方，我经常在这里买矿泉水、面包和咖啡。商店的东北角是卖手表的地方，我的手表就是在这里买的。卖电器的地方和这个方向相反，你可以在那里买到非常便宜的电视机。这里的衣服也很便宜。想买衣服的话，你进了南门往左拐，右边就是。

生词	Shēngcí	**New Words**		
1. 平面图	píngmiàntú	N	plane figure
2. 南门	nánmén	N	south gate
3. 进去	jìnqu	V	to enter
4. 经常	jīngcháng	Adv	often
5. 矿泉水	kuàngquánshuǐ	N	mineral water
6. 东北角	dōngběi jiǎo		northeast corner
7. 手表	shǒubiǎo	N	watch
8. 电器	diànqì	N	(household) electrical appliance
9. 方向	fāngxiàng	N	direction
10. 相反	xiāngfǎn	Adj	opposite
11. 电视机	diànshìjī	N	television

请在下图中填出卖吃的、卖手表、卖电器和卖衣服的地方。

Fill in the map according to the above passage.

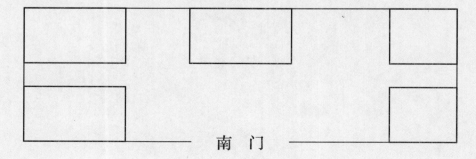

十三 谈谈你住的地方。

Talk about the place where you live.

提示：你住在哪儿？你住的地方附近有什么？你的房间在几层？你的房间里有什么？沙
　　　发在哪儿？电视在哪儿？介绍一下房间里你工作和学习的地方。

要求：用上"有"和"在"。

Prompt: Where do you live? What are there near your residence? Which floor is your room in? What are there in your room? Where is the sofa? Where is the TV set? Talk about the place where you work and study in the room.

Requirement: You need to use "有" and "在" in your passage.

十四 完成任务：请用课文中学过的词语和句子完成任务。

Complete the tasks: Please complete the tasks with the words and sentences you have learned in the texts.

1. 请用课文里学过的表示方位的词语向老师和同学介绍一下你住的地方的位置。

   Talk about the location of your residence to your teacher and classmates with the words denoting locality you learned in the texts.

2. 请确定一个你想去的地方，然后向中国人了解怎么去。要求每个学生选择不同的地方，上课时向老师和同学介绍。

   Please name a place you want to go and ask a Chinese how to get there. Every student chooses a different place. Present the information you've got to your teacher and classmates in class.

第七单元
UNIT 7
请客和吃饭
Inviting somebody to dinner

今天我请客
I'll stand treat today

课文 Text	题目 Title	注释 Notes
一	最近他家正在打折呢 They are having a discount these days	1. 动词"请" The verb "请" 2. 语气助词"哇" The modal particle "哇" 3. "正在……呢" 4. 形容词"火" The adjective "火" 5. 双宾语句 A sentence with double objects
二	请点菜 Would you please order your meal	1. "不好意思" 2. 可能补语 Complement of possibility 3. 副词"还是" The adverb "还是" 4. "那就……" 5. "看着 +V" 6. "买单" 7. "AA（制）" 8. 结果补语 Complement of result 9. 语气助词"嘛" The modal particle "嘛"

Zuìjìn Tā Jiā Zhèngzài Dǎzhé ne

最近他家正在打折呢

They are having a discount these days

Kǎ'ěr xiǎng qǐng kèhù chī fàn, tā qǐng Zhāng Yuǎn tuījiàn yì jiā fànguǎn.

卡尔想请客户吃饭，他请张远推荐一家饭馆。

Karl wants to invite his client to dinner, and he asks Zhang Yuan to recommend a restaurant.

Kǎ'ěr: Wǒ xiǎng qǐng kèhù chī fàn. Nǐ juéde nǎ jiā fànguǎn búcuò?

● 卡尔： 我想请客户吃饭。你觉得哪家饭馆不错？

Karl: I want to invite my client to dinner. Which restaurant do you think is good?

Zhāng Yuǎn: Xuéxiào nánmén fùjìn yǒu jiā chuāncài cāntīng, tǐng hǎo de.

○ 张远： 学校南门附近有家川菜餐厅，挺好的。

Zhang Yuan: There is a Sichuan cuisine restaurant near the south gate of the school. It's pretty good.

Kǎ'ěr: Hǎo wa! Xiànzài hěn liúxíng chī chuāncài.

● 卡尔： 好哇！现在很流行吃川菜。

Karl: Great! Sichuan cuisine is very popular now.

Zhāng Yuǎn: Wǒ shì nàr de chángkè. Zuìjìn tā jiā zhèngzài dǎzhé ne.

○ 张远： 我是那儿的常客。最近他家正在打折呢。

Zhang Yuan: I am their regular customer, and they are having a discount these days.

Kǎ'ěr: Dǎ jǐ zhé?

● 卡尔： 打几折？

Karl: What's the discount?

Zhāng Yuǎn: Bā zhé. Tā jiā shēngyi hěn huǒ, děi yùdìng.

○ 张远： 八折。他家生意很火，得预订。

Zhang Yuan: 20% off. Their business is brisk, so you need to make a reservation.

Kǎ'ěr: Nǐ gàosu wǒ tā jiā de diànhuà hàomǎ ba.

● 卡尔： 你告诉我他家的电话号码吧。

Karl: Can you give me its telephone number?

Zhāng Yuǎn: Méi wèntí!

○ 张远： 没问题！

Zhang Yuan: No problem!

生词　Shēngcí　New Words

1. 正在	zhèngzài	Adv	in the process of
2. 打折	dǎ zhé	V//O	to give a discount
3. 吃饭	chī fàn	V O	to have a meal
4. 饭馆（儿）	fànguǎn(r)	N	restaurant
5. 不错	búcuò	Adj	not bad
6. 南门	nánmén	N	south gate
7. 川菜	chuāncài	N	Sichuan cuisine
8. 餐厅	cāntīng	N	restaurant
9. 哇	wa	MdPt	*a modal particle*
10. 流行	liúxíng	V	to be popular
11. 那儿	nàr	Pr	there
12. 常客	chángkè	N	regular customer
13. 折	zhé	N	discount

14. 火	huǒ	Adj	brisk, prosperous
15. 预订	yùdìng	V	to reserve
16. 电话	diànhuà	N	telephone
17. 号码	hàomǎ	N	number

注释 Zhùshì Notes

1 **我想请客户吃饭。** **I want to invite my client to dinner.**

"请"，动词，表示邀请。基本结构："请（V₁）+ sb. + V₂ + sth."。例如：

"请", a verb, means "to invite". The basic structure is "请（V₁）+ sb.+ V₂ + sth.". For example,

S	P		
Pr / N / NP	V₁（请）	sb.	V₂	sth.
他		老师	喝	咖啡。
老板	请	我	吃	法国菜。
中国朋友		我	去	看电影。

2 **好哇！** **Great!**

"哇"，语气助词，读"wa"，是"啊"受前一个字韵母或韵尾 u、ou、ao 影响而发生的音变。这时"啊"可写成"哇"，也可用原字。"好哇"，常用在答句中，对别人的建议和看法表示肯定、赞同。

The modal particle "哇" is pronounced as wa. It is an inflexion of "啊" under the influence of u, ou or ao, the vowel or tail vowel of the preceding word. In this case, "啊" can be written as "哇", or remain unchanged. "好哇" is often used to agree with others' suggestion or idea.

3 **最近他家正在打折呢。** **They are having a discount these days.**

"正在……呢"，也可说"正 / 在……呢"、"……呢"，表示动作在进行或是状态持续中，可用于现在、过去和将来。"呢"，语气助词，放在句末，表示动作或状态正在进行。例如：

"正在……呢" indicates an action or a state is going on, and it can be used in present, past or future tense. The modal particle "呢" used at the end of the sentence indicates something is going on. Similar expressions are "正 / 在……呢", "……呢". For example,

① 他正在学习呢。

② 昨天晚上 12 点，我们正在聊天儿呢。

③ 明年（míngnián, next year）的这个时候，我可能正在工作呢。

④ 别说话！我们正开会呢。

⑤ 他们在吃饭呢。

⑥ 我帮卡尔找书呢。

4 他家生意很火。 **Their business is brisk.**

"火"，这里是形容词，指"兴旺，兴隆"，说明生意做得很好等。这句话的意思是："这家饭馆的生意很好"。例如：

"火", an adjective, means "brisk, prosperous". It indicates the business is very good. This sentence means "这家饭馆的生意很好". For example,

① 那家咖啡馆（kāfēiguǎn, cafe）的生意很火。

② 学校附近的肯德基（Kěndéjī, KFC）生意很火。

③ 这部电影很火。

5 你告诉我他家的电话号码吧。 **Can you give me its telephone number?**

双宾语句。基本结构："S + V + O₁ (sb.)+ O₂（sth.）"。汉语中可以带双宾语的动词不多，主要有"送"、"给"、"告诉"、"借（jiè, to borrow, to lend）"、"卖"、"还（huán, to return）"、"问"、"找"、"教（jiāo，to teach）"等。例如：

The basic pattern of a sentence with double objects is: "S + V + O₁ (sb.) + O₂ (sth.)". In Chinese, there are not many verbs that can be followed by two objects. The verbs that can take two objects include "送", "给", "告诉", "借", "卖", "还", "问", "找", "教", etc. For example,

S	P		
	V	O₁（sb.）	O₂（sth.）
他	送了	我	一本书。
我	借了	朋友	一百块钱。
张老师	教	我们	口语。

Qǐng Diǎn Cài
请点菜
Would you please order your meal

Zhāng Yuǎn: Jīntiān zánmen yìqǐ qù chī fàn ba, wǒ qǐngkè.
● 张远： 今天咱们一起去吃饭吧，我请客。
Zhang Yuan: Let's go to dinner. My treat today.

Kāng Àilì、Kǎ'ěr: Hǎo wa!
○ 康爱丽、卡尔： 好哇！
Alice and Karl: OK!

Lǐ Míngming: Bù hǎoyìsi, jīntiān wǒ yǒu shìr, nǐmen qù ba.
● 李明明： 不好意思，今天我有事儿，你们去吧。
Li Mingming: I'm sorry, but I have something to do. Enjoy yourselves.

Zài fànguǎn li.
在饭馆里。
In the restaurant.

Fúwùyuán: Zhè shì càidān, qǐng diǎn cài.
○ 服务员： 这是菜单，请点菜。
Waitress: Here is the menu. Would you please order your meal?

Kāng Àilì: Wǒ kàn bu dǒng, háishi nǐmen diǎn ba.

● 康爱丽: 我看不懂，还是你们点吧。

Alice: I can't read it. You order, please.

Zhāng Yuǎn: Nǐmen néng chī là de ma?

○ 张远: 你们能吃辣的吗？

Zhang Yuan: Can you eat spicy food?

Kāng Àilì: Wǒ bù xǐhuan chī là de, yě bù xǐhuan chī yóunì de.

● 康爱丽: 我不喜欢吃辣的，也不喜欢吃油腻的。

Alice: I don't like spicy food. Neither do I like greasy food.

Zhāng Yuǎn: Nǐ chīsù ma?

○ 张远: 你吃素吗？

Zhang Yuan: Are you a vegetarian?

Kāng Àilì: Bù chīsù. Jīròu、zhūròu、niúròu、yángròu, wǒ dōu chī.

● 康爱丽: 不吃素。鸡肉、猪肉、牛肉、羊肉，我都吃。

Alice: No. Chicken, pork, beef and mutton are OK for me.

Kǎ'ěr: Suān de、tián de、là de, wǒ dōu néng chī.

○ 卡尔: 酸的、甜的、辣的，我都能吃。

Karl: Sour, sweet and spicy foods are all OK for me.

Zhāng Yuǎn: Nà jiù lái yí fèn ròucài、yí fèn shūcài、yì tiáo yú, zài lái yí ge tāng,

● 张远: 那就来一份肉菜、一份蔬菜、一条鱼，再来一个汤，

zěnmeyàng?

怎么样？

Zhang Yuan: Then how about a meat dish, a vegetable, a fish, and a soup?

Kāng Àilì: Hǎo, nǐ kànzhe diǎn ba.

○ 康爱丽: 好，你看着点吧。

Alice: OK, it's up to you.

Zhāng Yuǎn gàosu fúwùyuán yào diǎn de cài.
张远告诉服务员要点的菜。
Zhang Yuan tells the waiter their order.

Fúwùyuán: Nǐmen yǒu shénme jìkǒu de ma?

● 服务员: 你们有什么忌口的吗？

Waitress: Do you avoid certain food?

Zhāng Yuǎn、Kāng Àilì、Kǎ'ěr: Méiyǒu.
○ 张远、康爱丽、卡尔:　　　没有。
Zhang Yuan, Alice and Karl:　　No.

Zhāng Yuǎn: Nǐmen hē shénme yǐnliào?
● 张远:　　你们喝什么饮料?
Zhang Yuan: What would you like to drink?

Kǎ'ěr:　　Lái liǎng píng píjiǔ.
○ 卡尔:　　来两瓶啤酒。
Karl:　　Two bottles of beer.

Kāng Àilì:　　Wǒ yào yì bēi guǒzhī.
● 康爱丽:　　我要一杯果汁。
Alice:　　I'd like a glass of juice.

Fúwùyuán: Yào zhǔshí ma?
○ 服务员:　　要主食吗?
Waitress:　　Any staple food?

Kāng Àilì:　　Yǒu dànchǎofàn ma?
● 康爱丽:　　有蛋炒饭吗?
Alice:　　Do you have fried rice with eggs?

Fúwùyuán:　　Yǒu.
○ 服务员:　　有。
Waitress:　　Yes, we do.

Kǎ'ěr:　　Wǒ yào yì wǎn mǐfàn.
● 卡尔:　　我要一碗米饭。
Karl:　　I'd like a bowl of rice.

Zhāng Yuǎn: Hǎo, yí fèn dànchǎofàn, liǎng wǎn mǐfàn.
○ 张远:　　好,一份蛋炒饭,两碗米饭。
Zhang Yuan: OK. A fried rice with eggs and two bowls of rice.

Chīwán fàn.
吃完饭。
After dinner.

Zhāng Yuǎn: Fúwùyuán, mǎidān!
● 张远:　　服务员,买单!
Zhang Yuan: Bill, please!

Kāng Àilì: Nǐ tài pòfèi le! Zánmen háishi AA ba.

○ 康爱丽： 你太破费了！咱们还是 AA 吧。

Alice: You shouldn't go to such expense. Let's go Dutch!

Zhāng Yuǎn: Shuōhǎole wǒ qǐngkè ma.

● 张远： 说好了我请客嘛。

Zhang Yuan: No, we have agreed it is my treat.

Kāng Àilì: Xièxie nǐ! Xià cì wǒ qǐng nǐmen chī Fǎguó cài.

○ 康爱丽： 谢谢你！下次我请你们吃法国菜。

Alice: Thank you! I'll treat you French dish next time.

Kǎ'ěr: Wǒ qǐng nǐmen qù Kǎibīnsījī Fàndiàn hē zhèngzōng de Déguó píjiǔ.

● 卡尔： 我请你们去凯宾斯基饭店喝正宗的德国啤酒。

Karl: I will treat you the authentic German beer in Kempinski Hotel.

生词　Shēngcí　**New Words**

1. 点	diǎn	V	to order (dishes)
2. 菜	cài	N	dish
3. 一起	yìqǐ	Adv	together
4. 请客	qǐng kè	V//O	to invite sb. to dinner
5. 不好意思	bù hǎoyìsi	IE	to be sorry
6. 服务员	fúwùyuán	N	waiter / waitress
7. 菜单	càidān	N	menu
8. 懂	dǒng	V	to understand
9. 还是	háishi	Adv	(*expressing hope*) had better
10. 辣	là	Adj	hot, spicy
11. 喜欢	xǐhuan	V	to like
12. 油腻	yóunì	Adj	oily, greasy
13. 吃素	chīsù	V	to be a vegetarian

14. 鸡肉	jīròu	N	chicken
15. 猪肉	zhūròu	N	pork
16. 牛肉	niúròu	N	beef
17. 羊肉	yángròu	N	mutton
18. 酸	suān	Adj	sour
19. 甜	tián	Adj	sweet
20. 份	fèn	M	*a measure word*
21. 肉	ròu	N	meat
22. 蔬菜	shūcài	N	vegetable
23. 条	tiáo	M	*a measure word*
24. 鱼	yú	N	fish
25. 汤	tāng	N	soup
26. 忌口	jì kǒu	V//O	to avoid certain food
27. 喝	hē	V	to drink
28. 饮料	yǐnliào	N	drink, beverage
29. 瓶	píng	N	bottle
30. 啤酒	píjiǔ	N	beer
31. 杯	bēi	N	cup, glass
32. 果汁	guǒzhī	N	juice
33. 主食	zhǔshí	N	staple food
34. 蛋炒饭	dànchǎofàn	N	fried rice with eggs
35. 碗	wǎn	N	bowl
36. 米饭	mǐfàn	N	cooked rice
37. 买单	mǎidān	V	to pay the bill
38. 破费	pòfèi	V	to go to such expense
39. 嘛	ma	MdPt	*a modal particle expressing that the situation is obvious*
40. 下	xià	N	next

| 41. 次 | cì | M | time |
| 42. 正宗 | zhèngzōng | Adj | authentic |

专有名词 Zhuānyǒu Míngcí **A Proper Noun**

| 凯宾斯基饭店 | Kǎibīnsījī Fàndiàn | Kempinski Hotel |

注释 Zhùshì **Notes**

1 不好意思，今天我有事儿，你们去吧。

I'm sorry, but I have something to do. Enjoy yourselves.

"不好意思"，有"对不起"的意思。口语中可用来表示抱歉或遗憾，语气比较委婉。

"不好意思" means "to be sorry". In oral Chinese, it can be used to show apology or regret in a mild tone.

2 我看不懂，还是你们点吧。 I can't read it. You order, please.

可能补语。在动词"看"和结果补语"懂"之间插入"得"或"不"就构成了可能补语，表示主观或客观条件是否允许某种情况发生。例如：

A complement of possibility is formed by inserting "得" or "不" between the verb "看" and the complement of result "懂". It indicates whether the subjective or objective condition allows a certain situation to happen. For example,

动词+结果补语 V + Complement of result	动词+可能补语 V + Complement of possibility	
	肯定式 Affirmative form	否定式 Negative form
看见	看得见	看不见
听清楚	听得清楚	听不清楚
说明白	说得明白	说不明白
进来	进得来	进不来

3 我看不懂，还是你们点吧。 I can't read it. You order, please.

"还是"，副词，表示经过比较、考虑后的选择，用"还是"引出决定选择的内容。"还是"引导的后一句的主语可以省略。例如：

The adverb "还是" indicates the choice is made after comparison or consideration. "还是" is followed by the choice made and the subject in the latter clause can be omitted. For example,

① 日本（Rìběn, Japan）菜太贵了，我们还是去吃中国菜吧。

② 天气冷了，还是多穿点儿吧。

③ 坐火车太慢了，咱们还是坐飞机去吧。

4 那就来一份肉菜、一份蔬菜、一条鱼，再来一个汤，怎么样？

Then how about a meat dish, a vegetable, a fish, and a soup?

"那"，连词，表示顺着前面句子的意思，作出判断或引出应有的结果。"那"放在句首，起承上的连接作用。"就"，副词，也表示承接前面说过的话，得出结论。主语可放在"那"后"就"前，也可省略。例如：

The conjunction "那" is used to introduce a judgment or a result based on the meaning of the preceding sentence. It is used at the beginning of a sentence to connect with the preceding sentence. The adverb "就" is also used to reach a conclusion following what was said before. The subject is used between "那" and "就" or omitted. For example,

① A: 他不喜欢吃苹果。

　　B: 那（我）就买香蕉吧。

② A: 我们已经去过长城了。

　　B: 那（我们）就去故宫（Gù Gōng, the Imperial Palace）。

③ A: 康经理，王经理来了。

　　B: 那就请他进来吧。

5 你看着点吧。 It's up to you.

"看着+动词"，习惯用法，意思是根据当时的情况去做某事。有时在句末加上"吧"，使语气较为舒缓。例如：

"看着 + V" is an idiom, meaning that doing something according to the actual situation. Sometimes "吧" is added at the end of the sentence to soften the tone. For example,

① 你看着办吧。

② 我看着买吧。

③ 你看着给吧。

6 服务员，买单！ Bill, please!

"买单"，指在饭馆里吃完饭后付钱，也可说"结账（jié zhàng）"，常用在口语中。原来是广东话"埋单（máidān）"，传到北方话地区后多说"买单"。现在也用在其他娱乐性消费中，如在 KTV、酒吧里结账等。

"买单" means paying the bill after finishing one's meal in a restaurant. "结账" is also often used in colloquial Chinese. "买单" originates from "埋单" in Cantonese, but "买单" is often used instead after this expression has spread to the north of China. Now it is also used when paying the bill for other recreational consumption, such as in KTV, bars, etc.

7 咱们还是AA吧。Let's go Dutch!

"AA"，又说"AA 制（zhì）"，表示在吃饭、娱乐等消费后各人付各人的钱或平分费用。对应于英语中的俗语"Let's go Dutch"。现在很多中国人，特别是年轻人都喜欢采用这种方式。

"AA" is also known as "AA 制". It means to pay one's own bill or share the cost after a meal or other recreational activities. It is equivalent to "Let's go Dutch" in English and is now a popular way of paying the bill among many Chinese, especially young people.

8 说好了我请客嘛。We have agreed it is my treat.

结果补语。形容词"好"放在动词后表示动作的完成，是动词"说"的结果补语。结果补语主要表示动作或状态的结果。可以作结果补语的有形容词、动词。

Complement of result. The adjective "好" is used after a verb to indicate the completion of the action. It is used as the complement of result of the verb "说". Complement of result is mainly used to indicate the result of an action or state. An adjective or a verb can be used as a complement of result.

结果补语和谓语动词之间不能插入其他成分，补语后可以用动态助词"了"，结果补语和"了"的后面可以有宾语。结果补语的否定式为"没 + 动词 + 结果补语"。例如：

No other element is inserted between a complement of result and a predicate verb. The aspect particle "了" is used after the complement. The complement of result and "了" can be followed by an object. The negative form of the complement of result is "没 + verb + complement of result". For example,

动词 + 结果补语　V + Complement of result	
肯定式　Affirmative form	否定式　Negative form
看见 / 听见 / 他看见了卡尔。	没看见 / 没听见 / 他没看见卡尔。
考完了 / 做完了 / 吃完了	没考完 / 没做完 / 没吃完
找到了 / 买到了	没找到 / 没买到
看懂了 / 听懂了	没看懂 / 没听懂
听清楚 / 说清楚	没听清楚 / 没说清楚
写对了 / 写错（cuò, wrong）了	没写对 / 没写错

9　**说好了我请客嘛。**　**We have agreed it is my treat.**

　　"嘛"，语气助词，读轻声，常用于口语，放在陈述句末尾，表示"很明显，事情就是如此"。句末语调用降调。

　　"嘛", a modal particle pronounced in the neutral tone, is often used in oral Chinese. It is usually put at the end of a declarative sentence, indicating that something is as it is be. A falling tone is used at the end of the sentence.

练习 Liànxí **Exercises**

一 跟读生词，注意发音和声调。
Read the new words after the teacher and pay attention to your pronunciation and tones.

二 跟读课文，注意语音语调。
Read the texts after the teacher and pay attention to your pronunciation and intonation.

三 学生分组，分角色朗读课文一、二。
Divide the students into groups and read Texts 1 & 2 in roles.

四 学生分组，不看书，分角色表演课文一、二。
Divide the students into groups and play the roles in Texts 1 & 2 without referring to the book.

五 角色扮演。（提示：角色可以互换。）
Role playing. (Note: the roles can be exchanged.)

1. 一位外国留学生 A 请中国朋友 B 给他推荐一家饭馆。
   An international student asked her Chinese friend to recommend a restaurant to him.

A	B
我想请朋友吃饭，你觉得哪家饭馆不错？	……
……	最近他家正在打折呢。
……	打八折。他家生意很火，得……
你告诉我他家的电话号码吧。	……

2. A 和 B 两人在一家饭馆点菜。
   A and B are ordering dishes in a restaurant.

A	B
你能吃辣的吗？	我不喜欢……，也不喜欢……。
来一个……，怎么样？	……
你有什么忌口吗？	……
来两瓶啤酒吧。	我要一杯……。
……	来两碗米饭。

3. 两人一组，根据下面的内容完成一段对话：你喜欢吃哪国菜？为什么？你吃过哪些中国菜？

Students work in pairs to complete a dialogue according to the following content: Which country's food do you like? Why? Which Chinese food have you had?

六 复述课文一和课文二。
Retell Texts 1 & 2.

七 替换练习。
Substitution drills.

① 我 想 请 <u>客户</u> <u>吃饭</u>。

卡尔	康爱丽	喝咖啡
康爱丽	老师	看电影
康爱丽	张远	吃法国菜
李明明	卡尔	唱歌

② 你觉得 <u>哪家饭馆</u> <u>不错</u>？

谁的汉语水平（shuǐpíng, level）	最高
什么时候去上海	合适
去超市怎么走	最近
谁的发音（fāyīn, pronunciation）	标准（biāozhǔn, standard）

③ <u>最近</u> <u>他家</u> 正在 <u>打折</u> 呢。

现在	卡尔	学习
昨天10点	康爱丽	跟朋友聊天儿
现在	张远	上网
早上8点	王老师	上课

④ 他家　生意　很火。

这家书店	书	很多
那家药店	药	很便宜
（yàodiàn, pharmacy）	（yào, medicine）	
那家咖啡馆	咖啡	很好喝
		（hǎohē, taste good）
这家饭馆	菜	很好吃
		（hǎochī, taste delicious）

⑤ 我看不懂，还是　你点　吧。

我不喜欢吃辣的	吃日本菜
我不喝啤酒	喝牛奶
我不想去商店	去书店
我不吃鸡肉	点牛肉

⑥ 我　不喜欢　吃　辣的，也不喜欢　吃　油腻的。

酸的	咸（xián, salty）的
甜的	苦的
牛肉	鸡肉
日本菜	韩国（Hánguó, Republic of Korea）菜

⑦ 那就　来　一份肉菜，再　来　一个汤，怎么样?

来	一瓶啤酒	来	一杯果汁
吃	一碗米饭	吃	一碗面条（miàntiáo, noodle）
吃	一个面包	喝	一杯牛奶
买	一件衬衣	买	一条裙子（qúnzi, skirt）

⑧ 咱们　还是　__AA__　吧。

一起去

坐飞机去

吃川菜

喝啤酒

八　用下面的词语组成句子。
Make sentences with the following words and expressions.

① 南门　川菜　附近　有　家　餐厅　学校

② 流行　川菜　很　现在　吃

③ 请客　我　今天

④ 忌口　什么　你们　有　吗　的

⑤ 你们　什么　点儿　喝　饮料

⑥ 能　辣　的　吗　你们　吃

⑦ 米饭　一　我　要　碗

⑧ 你　破费　太　了

⑨ 请客　我　好　说　了　嘛

⑩ 法国菜　次　请　我　你们　吃　下

九　阅读理解。
Reading comprehension.

周末的早上，我喜欢熬粥喝。一边听着音乐，一边喝着自己熬的香喷喷的粥，感觉棒极了。中午，我经常在家里煮面条。都说北方人爱吃面条，南方人爱吃米饭，我觉得一点儿也没错。有时候在家里吃腻了，我也会去外面的小饭馆换换口味。不过，我还是喜欢自己做饭吃，一来便宜，二来干净。去饭馆吃饭方便是方便，可是太吵了。人多的时候，还要等很长时间，肚子饿得咕咕叫，还不如在家吃呢。你呢？你喜欢在家里吃还是在外面吃？

生词 Shēngcí New Words

1. 熬	áo	V	to cook into porridge or soup
2. 粥	zhōu	N	porridge
3. 一边……一边……	yìbiān……yìbiān……		at the same time
4. 香喷喷	xiāngpēnpēn	Adj	delicious, savory, appetizing
5. 感觉	gǎnjué	V	to feel
6. 棒	bàng	Adj	good, excellent
7. 极	jí	Adv	extremely, to the greatest extent
8. 北方	běifāng	N	north
9. 爱	ài	V	to love, to be fond of, to like
10. 南方	nánfāng	N	south
11. 错	cuò	N	fault
12. 腻	nì	Adj	(be) fed up with
13. 换	huàn	V	to change
14. 口味	kǒuwèi	N	flavour or taste of food
15. 一来……二来……	yī lái……èr lái……		on one hand…on the other hand…
16. 吵	chǎo	Adj	noisy
17. 肚子	dùzi	N	belly, abdomen
18. 咕咕	gūgū	Ono	clucking of a hen, turtledove, etc.
19. 叫	jiào	V	to cry, to shout
20. 不如	bùrú	V	not as good as, would better

回答问题：

Answer the quetions：

① "我"喜欢早上吃什么？中午吃什么？

② "我"是哪儿人？

③ "我"总在家里吃吗？

④ "我"为什么喜欢自己做饭吃？

⑤ 你会做饭吗？你喜欢在哪儿吃？

 完成任务：请用课文中学过的词语和句子完成任务。

Complete the tasks: Please complete the tasks with the words and sentences you have learned in the texts.

1. 在中国，你去过哪些饭馆？那儿的菜怎么样？请在课堂上给大家介绍介绍。

 Which restaurants have you been to in China? How was the food there? Make a presentation to your teacher and classmates in class.

2. 请中国朋友推荐一家饭馆，去那里吃饭并了解情况。请注意：（1）你的朋友是怎么介绍的；（2）去那家饭馆后，服务员和你们是怎么对话的。请仔细观察这些情况，并把吃饭过程中的一些对话记录下来，然后到课堂上给大家介绍。

 Ask your Chinese friend to recommend a restaurant to you. Have a meal there and know more about it. Please note: (1) How did your friend recommend it? (2) After you got to the restaurant, how did the waiter talk to you? Observe carefully and write down the conversations you had while you were having the meal, then make a presentation in class.

第八单元
UNIT **8**
打电话
Making a telephone call

请问，林总经理在吗
Hello, may I speak to General Manager Lin

课文 Text	题目 Title	注释 Notes
一	您的电话号码是多少 Can I have your telephone number	1. 能愿动词"可以"　The optative verb "可以" 2. 复合趋向补语 　 Compound complement of direction 3. 电话号码的读法 　 The pronunciation of telephone numbers
二	后天您有空儿吗 Are you free the day after tomorrow	1. 连动句　A sentence with serial verbs 2. 副词"正好"　The adverb "正好" 3. 离合词　Verb-object compound 4. 连词"不过"　The conjunction "不过" 5. 主谓谓语句 　 A subject-predicate predicate sentence 6. 名词"时候"　The noun "时候" 7. 指示代词"这么" 　 The demonstrative pronoun "这么" 8. 习惯用语"那就这么定了" 　 The idiom "那就这么定了"
三	你有什么事儿吗 What's up	1. "哪位" 2. 疑问代词"怎么" 　 The interrogative pronoun "怎么" 　 辨析："怎么"、"为什么" 　 Discrimination: "怎么" and "为什么" 3. 疑问代词的虚指用法 　 Usage of indefinite reference of some interrogative pronouns 4. 动态助词"过"　The aspect particle "过" 5. "还没……呢"

6. 动词"随便"　The verb "随便"
7. 主谓短语作宾语
　　A subject-predicate phrase acts as an object
8. 12 星座　12 Zodiac Signs
9. 副词"最"　The adverb "最"
10. 叹词"嗯"　The interjection "嗯"
11. 能愿动词"应该"、"会"
　　The optative verbs "应该" and "会"
12. 语气助词"的"　The modal particle "的"
13. 插入语"对了"　The parenthesis "对了"
14. 习惯用语"就行"　The idiom "就行"
15. 习惯用语"那就这样"
　　The idiom "那就这样"

Nín de Diànhuà Hàomǎ Shì Duōshao

您的电话号码是多少

Can I have your telephone number

Lín Lín shì Jīnlóng Gōngsī de zǒngjīnglǐ, yě shì Kǎ'ěr gōngsī de kèhù. Kǎ'ěr zài gěi tā dǎ diànhuà.

林琳是金龙公司的总经理，也是卡尔公司的客户。
卡尔在给她打电话。

Lin Lin is the General Manager of Golden Dragon Company and is also a client of Karl's company. Karl is calling her.

Mìshū: Wèi, nín hǎo! Jīnlóng Gōngsī.

● 秘书：   喂，您好！金龙公司。

Secretary: Hello! Golden Dragon Company.

Kǎ'ěr: Nín hǎo! Qǐngwèn, Lín zǒngjīnglǐ zài ma?

○ 卡尔：   您好！请问，林总经理在吗？

Karl: Hello! Is General Manager Lin there?

Mìshū: Tā bú zài. Nín yǒu shìr ma? Wǒ kěyǐ bāng nín liúyán.

● 秘书：   她不在。您有事儿吗？我可以帮您留言。

Secretary: She is not in. Can I take a message?

Kǎ'ěr: Wǒ shì Kǎ'ěr, tā zhīdao. Qǐng tā huílai hòu gěi wǒ huí ge diànhuà.

○ 卡尔： 我是卡尔，她知道。请她回来后给我回个电话。

Karl: This is Karl, and she knows me. Please ask her to call me back when she is back.

Mìshū: Qǐngwèn, nín de diànhuà hàomǎ shì duōshao?

● 秘书： 请问，您的电话号码是多少？

Secretary: Excuse me, can I have your telephone number?

Kǎ'ěr: Liù jiǔ jiǔ jiǔ èr èr èr èr. Xièxie! Zàijiàn!

○ 卡尔： 69992222。谢谢！再见！

Karl: 69992222. Thank you! Goodbye!

Mìshū: Bú kèqi! Zàijiàn!

● 秘书： 不客气！再见！

Secretary: You are welcome! Goodbye!

生词　Shēngcí　**New Words**

1. 秘书	mìshū	N	secretary
2. 喂	wèi	Int	hello (used when making a phone call)
3. 总经理	zǒngjīnglǐ	N	general manager
4. 留言	liú yán	V//O	to leave a message
5. 回来	huílai	V	to be back, to return
6. 回	huí	V	to return, to reply

专有名词　Zhuānyǒu Míngcí　**Proper Nouns**

1. 金龙公司	Jīnlóng Gōngsī		name of a company
2. 林	Lín		a surname

注释 Zhùshì **Notes**

1 我可以帮您留言。Can I take a message?

"可以"，能愿动词，表示主观、客观以及情理上的许可。用在陈述句中，否定句中用"不能"，不说"不可以"。例如：

The optative verb "可以" indicates subjective or objective permission or permission based on common sense. Its negative form is "不能", not "不可以". For example,

① 我可以帮你学英语。

② 这个房间很大，可以住三个人。

③ 教室里不能吸烟（ xī yān, to smoke ），教室外面可以吸烟。

"可以"单独回答问题时，否定形式用"不行、不成"。例如：

"可以" can be used as an answer by itself. Its negative answer is "不行" or "不成". For example,

④ A：这儿可以吸烟吗？

　　B：可以。/ 不行。

2 请她回来后给我回个电话。Please ask her to call me back when she is back.

"回来"，复合趋向补语。趋向动词"来、去"放在一些动词后作补语，表示动作的趋向，构成复合趋向补语。常用的复合趋向补语有：

"回来" is a compound directional complement. The verb "来" or "去" is used after some verbs as a complement to indicate the direction of the action and form the complement of direction. The frequently used complements of direction are:

	上	下	进	出	回	过	开	到	起
来	上来	下来	进来	出来	回来	过来	开来	到……来	起来
去	上去	下去	进去	出去	回去	过去	开去	到……去	/

"来"表示动作向着说话人或所说的事物的方向移动；"去"表示动作离开说话人或所说的事物的方向，向另一个方向移动。例如：

"来" indicates to come towards the speaker or the thing mentioned; "去" means to go away from the speaker or the thing mentioned. For example,

① 这就是我的房间，进来吧。（说话人在房间里　The speaker is in the room. ）

② 这就是我的房间，进去吧。（说话人在房间外　The speaker is outside the room. ）

③ 教室在四层，我们上去吧。（说话人在楼下　The speaker is downstairs.）

④ 教室在四层，你们上来吧。（说话人已经在四层　The speaker is on the fourth floor.）

⑤ 卡尔到明明家去了。（说话人不在明明家，卡尔离开了说话人　The speaker is not at Mingming's home and Karl has left the speaker.）

⑥ 卡尔要到明明家来。（说话人在明明家　The speaker is at Mingming's home.）

当动词后面的宾语表示处所方位时，宾语要放在"来、去"的前面。例如：

If the object after the verb indicates place, it is used before "来" or "去". For example,

⑦ 我们进房间去吧。

⑧ 你们回家去。

⑨ 他跑回家来了。

⑩ 他搬（bān, to move）出学校的公寓去了。

⑪ 他走过马路去了。

⑫ 老师走进教室来了。

当动词后面的宾语表示人或事物时，宾语在"来、去"的前面和后面都可以。当宾语在"来、去"的后面时，往往表示动作已经完成。例如：

If the object after the verb refers to somebody or something, it can be used before or after "来" or "去". The object used after "来" or "去" often indicates the completion of an action. For example,

⑬ 他寄来了一本词典。/ 他寄了一本词典来。

⑭ 他拿来了一杯茶。/ 他拿了一杯茶来。

⑮ 明明带回来一只小狗（gǒu, dog）。/ 明明带回一只小狗来。

⑯ 卡尔送过来一本书。/ 卡尔送过一本书来。

⑰ 同学们举（jǔ, to lift, to raise）起手（shǒu, hand）来。

助词"了"可以放在谓语动词和补语之间，也可以放在补语"来、去"的后面。例如：

The particle "了" is put either between the predicate verb and the complement, or after the complement "来" or "去". For example,

⑱ 他送了三斤苹果来。/ 他送来了三斤苹果。

⑲ 他带了一位朋友来。/ 他带来了一位朋友。

⑳ 他给我发了一封邮件过来。/ 他给我发过来了一封邮件。

注意：当趋向补语放在句末，后面没有宾语时，通常要用复合趋向补语，"上、开"除外。当趋向补语后面有宾语或其他词语时，可以用简单趋向补语，也可以用复合趋向补语。例如：

Note: A compound directional complement is usually used if a directional complement is used at the end of a sentence and not followed by an object, except "上" and "开". If a directional complement is followed by an object or other words, a simple or compound directional complement is used. For example,

㉑有事儿，你就说出来。（√）

㉒有事儿，你就说出。（×）

㉓卡尔走进来了。

㉔卡尔走进教室了。

3 秘书：请问，您的电话号码是多少？卡尔：69992222。

Secretary: Excuse me, can I have your telephone number? Karl: 69992222.

电话号码的读法。如 64991345，读做 "liù sì jiǔ jiǔ yāo sān sì wǔ"。此外，房间、门牌、身份证、护照等的号码也是这样读。

The telephone number 64991345 is read as "liù sì jiǔ jiǔ yāo sān sì wǔ". Besides, the room numbers, doorplates, ID card numbers, and passport numbers are also read in the same way.

电话号码中的 "1"，习惯上读成 "yāo"；号码中的 "2" 读成 "èr"，不读 "liǎng"。

"1" in the telephone number is often read as "yāo" and "2" as "èr", not "liǎng".

120（yāo èr líng）——急救电话　First aid call

110（yāo yāo líng）——报警电话　Police call

119（yāo yāo jiǔ）——火警电话　Fire alarm call

Hòutiān Nín Yǒu Kòngr ma
后天您有空儿吗
Are you free the day after tomorrow

Lín Lín gěi Kǎ'ěr dǎ diànhuà.
林琳给卡尔打电话。
Lin Lin is giving Karl a phone call.

Kǎ'ěr: Wèi!
● 卡尔：   喂！
Karl: Hello!

Lín Lín: Wèi! Qǐngwèn, shì Kǎ'ěr xiānsheng ma?
○ 林琳：   喂！请问，是卡尔先生吗？
Lin Lin: Hello! Excuse me, is that Karl speaking?

Kǎ'ěr: Shì Lín zǒngjīnglǐ ba?
● 卡尔：   是林总经理吧？
Karl: Is that General Manager Lin?

Lín Lín: Shì wǒ. Nín shàngwǔ dǎ diànhuà zhǎo wǒ yǒu shìr ma?
○ 林琳：   是我。您上午打电话找我有事儿吗？
Lin Lin: Yes, this is she. You called me this morning, and is there anything I can do for
         you?

Kǎ'ěr: Lín zǒng, wǒ xiǎng míngtiān qǐng nín hē kāfēi, tán yi tán zánmen hézuò

● 卡尔： 林总，我想明天请您喝咖啡，谈一谈咱们合作

de xìjié, nín yǒu shíjiān ma?

的细节，您有时间吗？

Karl: General Manager Lin, I'd like to invite you to coffee tomorrow to talk about the details of our cooperation. Do you have time?

Lín Lín: Wǒ zhènghǎo yě xiǎng hé nín jiàn yí miàn. Búguò, míngtiān yì tiān wǒ dōu

○ 林琳： 我正好也想和您见一面。不过，明天一天我都

hěn máng.

很忙。

Lin Lin: I'm also thinking of meeting you sometime. But I'll be very busy the whole day tomorrow.

Kǎ'ěr: Nà nín shénme shíhou fāngbiàn?

● 卡尔： 那您什么时候方便？

Karl: Then when will you be available?

Lín Lín: Hòutiān nín yǒu kòngr ma?

○ 林琳： 后天您有空儿吗？

Lin Lin: Do you have time the day after tomorrow?

Kǎ'ěr: Yǒu kòngr! Gōngtǐ Běilù nàbiān yǒu yì jiā kāfēitīng hěn búcuò, wǒmen jiù

● 卡尔： 有空儿！工体北路那边有一家咖啡厅很不错，我们就

qù nàr, zěnmeyàng?

去那儿，怎么样？

Karl: Yes, I do. There is a wonderful coffee house on Gongti North Road. How about going there?

Lín Lín: Hǎo de, xiàwǔ liǎng diǎn bàn ba.

○ 林琳： 好的，下午两点半吧。

Lin Lin: OK. Can we meet at 2:30 in the afternoon?

Kǎ'ěr: Nà jiù zhème dìng le! Yíhuìr wǒ gěi nín fā duǎnxìn, gàosu nín dìzhǐ.

● 卡尔： 那就这么定了！一会儿我给您发短信，告诉您地址。

Karl: Then that's settled! I will send you a message to tell you the address later on.

Lín Lín: Hǎo.

○ 林琳： 好。

Lin Lin: OK.

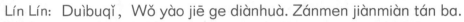

Zhèshí Lín Lín de lìng yí bù diànhuà xiǎng le.

这时林琳的另一部电话响了。

At the moment, Lin Lin's another telephone is ringing.

Lín Lín: Duìbuqǐ, Wǒ yào jiē ge diànhuà. Zánmen jiànmiàn tán ba.

○ 林琳： 对不起，我要接个电话。咱们见面谈吧。

Lin Lin: I am sorry, but I have a phone call to answer. Let's talk when we meet.

Kǎ'ěr: Hòutiān jiàn!

● 卡尔： 后天见！

Karl: See you the day after tomorrow.

生词 Shēngcí New Words

1.	后天	hòutiān	N	the day after tomorrow
2.	空儿	kòngr	N	free time
3.	打	dǎ	V	to make (a phone call)
4.	谈	tán	V	to talk
5.	合作	hézuò	V	to cooperate
6.	细节	xìjié	N	detail
7.	正好	zhènghǎo	Adv	happen to, just
8.	和	hé	Prep	and, with
9.	见面	jiàn miàn	V//O	to meet
10.	不过	búguò	Conj	but
11.	咖啡厅	kāfēitīng	N	cafe
12.	这么	zhème	Pr	so, such, this way, like this
13.	定	dìng	V	to settle, to decide
14.	一会儿	yíhuìr	Q	a little while
15.	短信	duǎnxìn	N	message
16.	地址	dìzhǐ	N	address

| 17. 接 | jiē | V | to receive |

专有名词 Zhuānyǒu míngcí **Proper Nouns**

| 1. 林琳 | Lín Lín | name of a person |
| 2. 工体北路 | Gōngtǐ Běilù | name of a road (Gongti is the abbreviation of the Worker's Gymnasium.) |

注释 Zhùshì **Notes**

1 **您上午打电话找我有事儿吗?**

You called me this morning, and is there anything I can do for you?

连动句。谓语由两个或两个以上的动词构成，几个动词短语共有一个主语。动词之间没有停顿，也没有关联词语。从意义上看，这些动词短语是事理上的或者自然的先后关系。本句话包括了三个动词短语："打电话"、"找我"、"有事儿"，它们的主语都是"你"。连动句的基本结构："S+ V_1P_1 + V_2P_2 + ……"。例如：

This is a sentence with serial verbs. In a sentence with serial verbs, the predicate is composed of two or more verbs which share the same subject, and there is not a pause nor connection words between them. From the semantic view, these verbs have a sequential relationship in sense and nature. There are three verbal phrases in this sentence: "打电话", "找我", "有事儿", which share the same subject "你". The basic structure is "S + V_1P_1 + V_2P_2 + …". For example,

S	P			
	TW/Adv	V_1P_1	V_2P_2	V_3P_3
您	上午	打电话	找我	有事儿吗?
我们	（一起）	去超市	买苹果。	
他们	（下个月）	来北京	学习汉语。	
他们		吃过早饭	去机场	接朋友了。
卡尔	昨晚	上网	找朋友	玩游戏。
康爱丽		坐飞机	去上海	见客户了。

注意：连动句中动词短语的位置一般是不能换的。

Note：Generally, the positions of the verbal phrases in a sentence with serial verbs cannnot be changed.

2 我正好也想和您见一面。 I'm also thinking of meeting you sometime.

"正好"，副词，表示两件事发生的时间很巧。例如：

The adverb "正好" indicates that two events happen at the same time by coincidence. For example,

① 我想去超市，她正好也想去，我们就一起去了超市。

② 我刚想给她打电话，正好她来了。

③ 我一直想去长城，可是没有时间，正好这两天放假(fàng jià, to have a vacation)可以去。

3 我正好也想和您见一面。 I'm also thinking of meeting you sometime.

"见面"，离合词。汉语中的离合词大多是动宾式的，离合词的后面一般不带宾语。例如：

"见面" is a verb-object compound. Most verb-object compounds in Chinese are formed by a verb and an object. Generally, a verb-object compound cannot take another object. For example,

① 我想见面你。（×）

② 我想见你一面。（√）

③ 我想和你见面。（√）

④ 他结婚(jié hūn, to marry)小王了。（×）

⑤ 他和小王结婚了。（√）

动宾式离合词的两个字之间可以插入其他词语。如"结过一次婚、洗了一次澡、见过一面"。这种结构的重叠形式是：AAB，如"唱唱歌、跳跳舞"等。

Other words can be used between the two characters of a verb-object compound. For example, "结过一次婚", "洗了一次澡", "见过一面". The reduplication form of this structure is: AAB, for example, "唱唱歌", "跳跳舞", etc.

4 不过，明天一天我都很忙。 But I'll be very busy the whole day tomorrow.

"不过"，连词，表示转折，用在后一分句的开头。表示后边的分句不是顺着前一分句的意思说下去的，而是发生了转折，变成了相反或者相对的意思。"不过"转折的程度比"但是、可是"轻一些，常用在口语里。例如：

The conjunction "不过" is used at the beginning of the second clause to indicate a transition. It indicates the second clause doesn't follow the meaning of the preceding clause, but there is some change into the opposite direction. The degree of transition "不过" indicates is lower than that "但是" or "可是" does and is often used in oral Chinese. For example,

clause 1	Conj (不过)	clause 2
今天天气不错，		有点儿冷。
这个菜很好吃，	不过	太贵了。
汉语有点儿难，		很有意思（yǒu yìsi，interesting）。

5 明天一天我都很忙。 **But I'll be very busy the whole day tomorrow.**

主谓谓语句，指主谓短语作谓语的句子。这是汉语特有的一种句子。主谓谓语句的谓语主要是描写或者说明主语的。

This is a subject-predicate predicate sentence. The subject-predicate predicate sentence is a sentence with a subject-predicate phrase as the predicate. This kind of sentences are unique in Chinese, and the predicate in such a sentence is mainly used to describe or explain the subject.

本句中，大主语是"明天一天"，大谓语是"我都很忙"；小主语是"我"，小谓语是"都很忙"。否定式是在主谓短语的谓语中加否定词"不"，如"明天一天我都不忙"。例如：

In this sentence, the major subject is "明天一天" and the major predicate "我都很忙". Its minor subject is "我" and minor predicate "都很忙". Its negative form is to place a negative word "不" between the minor subject and the minor predicate of the subject-predicate phrase, for example, "明天一天我都不忙". For example,

S₁	P₁	
	S₂	P₂
学校附近的超市	你	去过吗？
这个人	我	不认识。
这家饭馆的菜	我们	都很喜欢。

6 那您什么时候方便？ **Then when will you be available?**

"时候"，名词，指时间里的某一点或某一段。和疑问代词"什么"组成"什么时候"，用来询问时间。例如：

The noun "时候" indicates a certain point or a period of time. It forms "什么时候" with the interrogative pronoun "什么" and is used to inquire time. For example,

① 您什么时候有空儿？

② 你们什么时候考试？

③ 我们什么时候去吃饭？

7 那就这么定了！ Then that's settled!

"这么"，指示代词，指示性质、状态、方式、程度等，在句中只能作定语或状语。在口语中常常说成"zème"。例如：

The demonstrative pronoun "这么" indicates the characteristics, state, manner or degree, etc, and can only be used as an attribute or an adverbial in a sentence. It is often pronounced as "zème" in oral Chinese. For example,

① 同学们都这么说。

② 你的汉语这么好呀！

③ 这是真的，是有这么回（huí, *a measure word*）事儿。

8 那就这么定了！ Then that's settled!

习惯用语。跟别人商量事情以后，常说"那就这么定了"表示事情决定了，不再改变了。常用于计划或邀请、约会。"那"可以省略。例如：

It is an idiom. After discussing with others, we often say "那就这么定了", indicating that it is settled and will not be changed. It is often used when making a plan, sending an invitation, or making an appointment. "那" can be omitted. For example,

A：明天早上我来接你，九点钟在您家门口（ménkǒu, doorway）见。

B：好，（那）就这么定了。

你有什么事儿吗

What's up

Kāng Àilì gěi Kǎ'ěr dǎ diànhuà.
康爱丽给卡尔打电话。
Alice is giving Karl a phone call.

Kāng Àilì: Wèi, nǐ hǎo!
● 康爱丽：喂，你好！
Alice:　Hello!

Kǎ'ěr:　Wèi, nǐ hǎo! Nǎ wèi?
○ 卡尔：　喂，你好！哪位？
Karl:　Hello! Who is that?

Kāng Àilì: Kāng Àilì!
● 康爱丽：康爱丽！
Alice:　It's Alice.

Kǎ'ěr:　Àilì, shénme shìr?
○ 卡尔：　爱丽，什么事儿？
Karl:　Aili, what's up?

Kāng Àilì: Wǒ zuó wǎn gěi nǐ jiā dǎle hěn duō cì diànhuà, dōu méi rén jiē. Nǐ qù

● 康爱丽：我昨晚给你家打了很多次电话，都没人接。你去

nǎr le?

哪儿了？

Alice: I called your home phone several times last night, but there was no answer. Where did you go?

Kǎ'ěr: Nà nǐ zěnme bù dǎ wǒ shǒujī? Wǒ qù jiànle ge kèhù. Nǐ yǒu shénme

○ 卡尔：那你怎么不打我手机？我去见了个客户。你有什么

shìr ma?

事儿吗？

Karl: Why didn't you call my mobile phone? I went to see a client. What's up?

Kāng Àilì: Méi shénme jí shìr. Xià zhōu'èr shì Lǐ Míngming de shēngrì. Tā yào bàn

● 康爱丽：没什么急事儿。下周二是李明明的生日。她要办

ge shēngrì jùhuì, xiǎng qǐng nǐ cānjiā.

个生日聚会，想请你参加。

Alice: Nothing urgent. Next Tuesday is Li Mingming's birthday. She will hold a party and invite you to come.

Kǎ'ěr: Guò shēngrì? Hǎo a! Zài nǎr?

○ 卡尔：过生日？好啊！在哪儿？

Karl: Birthday party? Great! Where is it?

Kāng Àilì: Jiù zài tā zū de gōngyù li, tā qīnzì xià chú, ràng zánmen chángchang

● 康爱丽：就在她租的公寓里，她亲自下厨，让咱们尝尝

tā de jiāxiāng cài.

她的家乡菜。

Alice: Right in the apartment she rents. She will cook the meal herself and let us have a taste of her hometown dishes.

Kǎ'ěr: Tài hǎo le! Wǒ hái méi qù Zhōngguó rén jiāli zuòguo kè ne. Yào zhǔnbèi

○ 卡尔：太好了！我还没去中国人家里做过客呢。要准备

shénme lǐwù ma?

什么礼物吗？

Karl: Wonderful! I've never visited a Chinese family before. Shall we prepare some gifts?

Kāng Àilì: Suíbiàn nǐ.

● 康爱丽：随便你。

Alice: As you like.

Kǎ'ěr:　　Nà wǒ gěi tā dìng ge dàngāo ba.
○ 卡尔：　那我给她订个蛋糕吧。
Karl:　　Let me order a cake for her.

Kāng Àilì:　Tā yǐjīng dìngguo le.
● 康爱丽：她已经订过了。
Alice:　　She has already ordered one.

Kǎ'ěr:　　Nà nǐ zhīdao tā xǐhuan shénme ma?
○ 卡尔：　那你知道她喜欢什么吗？
Karl:　　Do you know what she likes?

Kāng Àilì:　Tā ya, Shuāngyú Zuò de, shì ge hěn làngmàn de rén, zuì xǐhuan huār le.
● 康爱丽：她呀，双鱼座的，是个很浪漫的人，最喜欢花儿了。
Alice:　　She, a Pisces, is very romantic. She likes flowers the most.

Kǎ'ěr:　　Sòng tā bǎihéhuā, zěnmeyàng?
○ 卡尔：　送她百合花，怎么样？
Karl:　　What about lilies?

Kāng Àilì:　Ǹg, Wǒ juéde tā yīnggāi huì hěn xǐhuan de.
● 康爱丽：嗯，我觉得她应该会很喜欢的。
Alice:　　Hum, I guess she will like them very much.

Kǎ'ěr:　　Duì le, nǐ zhīdao tā jiā zài nǎr ma? Zánmen zěnme qù?
○ 卡尔：　对了，你知道她家在哪儿吗？咱们怎么去？
Karl:　　By the way, do you know where she lives? How can we get there?

Kāng Àilì:　Tā jiā jiù zài xuéxiào pángbiān. Zánmen zhōu'èr xiàkè hòu zǒu guoqu
● 康爱丽：她家就在学校旁边。咱们周二下课后走过去
　　　　　jiù xíng.
　　　　　就行。
Alice:　　She lives near the school. We can walk there after class on Tuesday.

Kǎ'ěr:　　Nà jiù zhèyàng. Zàijiàn!
○ 卡尔：　那就这样。再见！
Karl:　　Then it's settled. See you!

Kāng Àilì:　Zàijiàn!
● 康爱丽：再见！
Alice:　　See you!

71

商务汉语系列教程·基础篇2

生词 Shēngcí **New Words**

1. 家	jiā	N	family, home
2. 手机	shǒujī	N	mobile phone
3. 生日	shēngrì	N	birthday
4. 办	bàn	V	to hold (a party, etc.)
5. 聚会	jùhuì	V/N	to get together; get-together, party
6. 参加	cānjiā	V	to take part in, to attend
7. 租	zū	V	to rent
8. 亲自	qīnzì	Adv	in person
9. 下厨	xià chú	V O	to cook
10. 让	ràng	V	to allow, to let
11. 家乡	jiāxiāng	N	hometown
12. 做客	zuò kè	V//O	to be a guest
13. 过	guo	AP	*used after a verb to indicate the completion of an action*
14. 礼物	lǐwù	N	gift
15. 随便	suí biàn	V//O	to do as one likes
16. 订	dìng	V	to order, to book
17. 蛋糕	dàngāo	N	cake
18. 浪漫	làngmàn	Adj	romantic
19. 最	zuì	Adv	most
20. 花儿	huār	N	flower
21. 百合	bǎihé	N	lily
22. 嗯	ǹg	Int	*expressing a positive answer*
23. 应该	yīnggāi	OpV	should, ought to
24. 会	huì	OpV	can, will
25. 这样	zhèyàng	Pr	this way

专有名词	*Zhuānyǒu Míngcí*	**A Proper Noun**
双鱼座	Shuāngyú Zuò	Pisces

注释 Zhùshì **Notes**

1 喂，你好！哪位？ **Hello! Who is that?**

"哪位"，用于接电话、应门铃时，询问对方是谁。例如：

"哪位" is used to ask the identity of the listener when answering a telephone or doorbell. For example,

① A：您是哪位？

B：我是康爱丽。

② A：哪位？

B：是我，康爱丽。

2 那你怎么不打我手机？ **Why didn't you call my mobile phone?**

"怎么"，疑问代词，这里用来询问原因。例如：

The interrogative pronoun "怎么" is used to ask the reason here. For example,

① 明明怎么哭（kū, to cry）了？

② 你怎么没去上课？

③ 他怎么能去？我怎么不能去？

在汉语中，用来询问原因还常用"为什么"。"为什么"是疑问代词"什么"和动词"为（wèi）"组成的动宾短语，放在动词、形容词的前面，可以用在句首或者句末。例如：

In Chinese, the interrogative pronoun "什么" often forms a verb-object phrase "为什么" with the verb "为". "为什么" is usually put before a verb or an adjective in a sentence to ask the reason. For example,

④ 你为什么迟到？

⑤ 为什么他不去上海？

⑥ 这是为什么？

辨析 Discrimination: "怎么"、"为什么"

用"怎么"询问原因时，问话人有明显的奇怪、诧异、惊讶的意思。而"为什么"主要是用来问原因。当问话人只是想知道答案，没有任何诧异的意思时，只能用"为什么"，如老师上课提问一般用"为什么"。例如：

When "怎么" is used to ask the reason, it indicates that the asker feels something is strange or the speaker is surprised at something. "为什么" is mainly used to ask the reason. When the asker only wants to know the answer and is not surprised, he can only use "为什么". For example, when the teacher raises a question in class, he generally uses "为什么". For example,

⑦ 这里为什么不能用"了"？

⑧ 你为什来中国学习汉语？

3 你有什么事儿吗？ What's up?/没什么急事儿。 Nothing urgent./
要准备什么礼物吗？ Shall we prepare some gifts?

"什么"，疑问代词，用于虚指，表示不确定、不具体的事物，不需要回答和说明。疑问代词"哪儿"、"怎么"、"谁"等也有同样的用法。例如：

The interrogative pronoun "什么" refers to an indefinite or unspecific thing. The speaker does not need an answer or explanation. Other interrogative pronouns, like "哪儿", "怎么", and "谁", etc., can also be used in this way. For example,

① 他想在北京买点儿什么送给他的朋友。

② 我在哪儿看到过这本书。

③ 你来的时候看见谁了吗？

4 我还没去中国人家里做过客呢。 I've never visited a Chinese family before.

"过"，动态助词，读轻声，表示某种行为或变化曾经发生，但并未继续到现在。曾经发生的动作或具有的状态是过去的经历。放在动词后、宾语前。表示否定时用"没（有）"。例如：

The aspect particle "过" is pronounced in the neutral tone. It indicates some action or change happened, but did not last. The action happened or the state existed in the past. It is used after a verb and before an object. It is negated by using "没（有）". For example,

我去过法国，但是没去过德国。

肯定句 Affirmative sentence	我去中国人家里做过客。
否定句 Negative sentence	我没去中国人家里做过客。
一般疑问句 General interrogative sentence	你去中国人家里做过客吗？

5 我还没去中国人家里做过客呢。I've never visited a Chinese family before.

"还没……呢"，用在陈述句中，表示强调事实，有时带有一些夸张。例如：

"还没……呢" in a declarative sentence is used to emphasize a fact, with a little bit exaggeration sometimes. For example,

① 我还没吃饭呢。

② 别着急（zháo jí, worried）！老师还没来呢。

③ 我还没见过这么漂亮（piàoliang, beautiful）的画儿呢！

6 随便你。 As you like.

"随便"，这里是动词，在口语中，常用来告诉对方按照自己的方便来做。也可以单独使用，如"随你的便"。

"随便", a verb, is usually used in oral Chinese to tell the listener to do something for his own convenience. It can also be used by itself, for example, "随你的便".

7 那你知道她喜欢什么吗?   Do you know what she likes?

主谓短语作宾语。"她喜欢什么"是主谓短语，作动词"知道"的宾语。全句的谓语动词大多表示心理活动或感觉，如"想、看到、觉得、知道"等。例如：

A subject-predicate phrase acts as an object. "她喜欢什么", subject-predicate phrase, is the object of the verb "知道". The predicate verb of the sentence is mostly used to indicate mental activitiy or feeling, for example, "想", "看到", "觉得", "知道", etc. For example,

① 你知道她家在哪儿吗?

② 我看到他今天下午去图书馆了。

8 她呀，双鱼座的，……   She, a Pisces, ...

"双鱼座",12星座之一。古代人把天空分为12个区域，用12个星座来计量时间，后来，人们用它来代表人的不同的性格特点。每个星座都有固定的时间段，人们可以根据自己的出生日期来确定自己属于哪个星座。具体的12星座见下表：

"双鱼座" (Pisces) is one of the 12 Zodiac Signs. Ancient people divided the sky into 12 areas and use 12 Zodiac Signs to measure time. Afterwards, people use them to represent different personalities of people. Each of the Zodiac Signs has its own fixed period of time. People can determine which Zodiac Signs they belong to according to their birth dates. The following table lists the 12 Zodiac Signs.

日期　Date	星座　Zodiac Sign	拼音　*Pinyin*	英文　English
3.21～4.19	白羊座	Báiyáng Zuò	Aries
4.20～5.20	金牛座	Jīnniú Zuò	Taurus
5.21～6.21	双子座	Shuāngzǐ Zuò	Gemini
6.22～7.22	巨蟹座	Jùxiè Zuò	Cancer
7.23～8.22	狮子座	Shīzi Zuò	Leo
8.23～9.22	处女座	Chǔnǚ Zuò	Virgo
9.23～10.23	天秤座	Tiānchèng Zuò	Libra
10.24～11.22	天蝎座	Tiānxiē Zuò	Scorpio
11.23～12.21	射手座	Shèshǒu Zuò	Sagittarius
12.22～1.19	摩羯座	Mójié Zuò	Capricorn
1.20～2.18	水瓶座	Shuǐpíng Zuò	Aquarius
2.19～3.20	双鱼座	Shuāngyú Zuò	Pisces

9 **最喜欢花儿了。She likes flowers the most.**

"最"，副词，表示程度，是程度的最高级，意思是在某方面超过了所有同类的人或事物。可以放在形容词、能愿动词和表示心理状态的动词（如"喜欢"）前。例如：

The adverb "最" indicates the superlative degree, meaning it surpasses all the persons or things of the same type. It can be used before an adjective, an optative verb and a verb indicating mental activity (such as "喜欢"). For example,

最	快/好/便宜（Adj）
	想去上海（OpV）
	喜欢北京（V）

① 最快：坐什么车去学校最快？
② 最好：我什么时候去你家最好？
③ 最好吃：学校附近哪家饭馆最好吃？
④ 最便宜：哪家超市的东西最便宜？

10 **嗯，我觉得她应该会很喜欢的。Hum, I guess she will like them very much.**

"嗯"，叹词，读 ńg，表示肯定的应答。这句是"我"对"她"喜欢这份礼物这种可能情况的估计。

The interjection "嗯" indicates an affirmative reply. In this sentence, "我" (I) guess "她" (she) will like the gift.

11　**我觉得她应该会很喜欢的。I guess she will like them very much.**

"应该"，能愿动词，可以表示事实上或情理上的许可，也可以表示推测或估计。可以用在书面语中，也可以用在口语中。例如：

"应该", an optative verb, indicates permission, speculation or estimation. It can be used in both written and spoken Chinese. For example,

① 你不应该迟到。（表示许可　To indicate permission.）

② 已经七点了，他们应该来了。（表示估计　To indicate estimation.）

"会"，能愿动词，表示有可能实现。过去和将来的情况都可以用。例如：

"会", an optative verb, indicates a possible realization. It can be used both in past tense and in future tense. For example,

③ 我真没想到你会来。

④ 明天早上我会送她去机场的。

只要意义上许可，能愿动词可以连用。例如：

As long as it is allowed semantically, the optative verbs can be used together. For example,

⑤ 我明天可能要去上海。

⑥ 他应该会写这些汉字。

12　**我觉得她应该会很喜欢的。I guess she will like them very much.**

"的"，语气助词，用在陈述句中，表示情况本来如此，加强肯定的语气。例如：

The modal particle "的" is used in a declarative sentence to indicate the situation is as expected. It is used to strengthen the tone. For example,

① 她一定（yí dìng, to be sure to）会喜欢的。

② 你放心（fàng xīn, to set one's mind at rest），我们会去的。

③ 他应该会知道的。

13　**对了，你知道她家在哪儿吗？　By the way, do you know where she lives?**

"对了"，插入语。这里表示在说话的过程中忽然想起了别的事情。

The parenthesis "对了" indicates something else suddenly occurs to the speaker's mind when he is speaking.

口语中，说话人常用"对了"来引起对方的注意，表示自己下面要说某些忽然想起来的事情，这可以是原来不太清楚或一时忘了的事情，也可以是临时想起来的事情。

In oral Chinese, the speaker often uses "对了" to arouse the listener's attention, indicating he is going to say something that he wasn't clear about before or forgot, or things that suddenly occurs to his mind.

14 咱们周二下课后走过去就行。**We can walk there after class on Tuesday.**

"就行"，常用在句末，表示对这句话的肯定。"就"，副词，表示在某种条件或情况下自然会怎么样。"行"，动词，"可以"的意思。"就行"也可以说"就可以"。例如：

"就行" is often used at the end of the sentence to confirm the sentence. "就", an adverb, indicates that the thing will naturally turn out in some way under certain condition or situation. "行", a verb, means "can". "就可以" can also be used instead. For example,

① 来中国旅游（lǚyóu, to travel），你会说一些生活汉语就行。

② 我们两个人去就行，你不用去了。

③ 我们走着去就可以，不用坐出租车。

15 那就这样。 **Then it's settled.**

"那就这样"，习惯用语。副词"就"表示确定范围，"就这样"是固定的用法，表示没有其他情况。"那就这样"表示根据上文得出结论，并确定这一结论。当双方已经达成了一致的意见，另一方在结束双方的谈话前用这句话表示对事情的确定。可以在句中单独使用。例如：

"那就这样" is an idiom. The adverb "就" indicates a certain scope. "就这样" is a fixed expression, denoting there is no other situation. "那就这样" indicates a conclusion is reached and conformed based on the previous context. If both sides have reached an agreement, one of them can use this sentence to show his confirmation before the conversation ends. It can be used on its own in a sentence. For example,

A：我们明天一起去长城吧。

B：好的。

A：那就这样，明天见。

练习 Liànxí **Exercises**

一 跟读生词，注意发音和声调。
Read the new words after the teacher and pay attention to your pronunciation and tones.

二 跟读课文，注意语音语调。
Read the texts after the teacher and pay attention to your pronunciation and intonation.

三 学生分组，分角色朗读课文一、二、三。
Divide the students into groups and read Texts 1, 2 & 3 in roles.

四 学生分组，不看书，分角色表演课文一、二。
Divide the students into groups and play the roles in Texts 1 & 2 without referring to the book.

五 角色扮演。（提示：角色可以互换。）
Role playing. (Note: the roles can be exchanged.)

1. 在教室里，简单布置一个办公环境，三个学生一组，分别扮演总经理、秘书、客户，模拟客户打电话，秘书接电话、留言，总经理回电话等情景。
In the classroom, set up a simple office environment . Students are divided into groups of three and act as if the client is making a call, the secretary is answering the phone and taking the message, and the General Manager is answering back.

2. 三个学生一组，学生 A 首先介绍自己的生日、星座、喜欢什么生日礼物等，然后学生 B 和 C 打电话商量送 A 什么生日礼物、去哪儿庆祝生日等。
Students are divided into groups of three. Firstly, Student A tells his birthday, constellation and birthday present he likes. Then, students B and C discuss on phone what they will give A for his birthday and where they will celebrate his birthday.

六 复述课文三。
Retell Text 3.

七 把动词和它的宾语用线连起来。

Connect the verbs and their corresponding objects.

发　　　　　　　　　　　　　　　事情

打　　　　　　　　　　　　　　　客户

订　　　　　　　　　　　　　　　机票

谈　　　　　　　　　　　　　　　短信

尝　　　　　　　　　　　　　　　公寓

租　　　　　　　　　　　　　　　聚会

约见（yuējiàn, to make an appointment）　电话

参加　　　　　　　　　　　　　　家乡菜

八 替换练习。

Substitution drills.

① 我　可以　帮　你　留言。

秘书	客户	发传真（chuánzhēn, fax）
小王	你们	订机票
老师	同学们	买语法书
康爱丽	我们	问问这件事儿

② 请　她　回来后　给　我　回个电话。

卡尔	到北京后	小王	打个电话
秘书	周末	客户	发传真
班长（bānzhǎng, class monitor）	下次上课前	同学们	讲讲这件事儿
小王	聚会时	我们	唱歌

❸ 请问，您的 <u>电话</u> 号码 是多少？

> 传真
>
> 房间
>
> 护照（hùzhào, passport）
>
> 身份证（shēnfènzhèng, ID card）

❹ <u>卡尔</u> <u>上午</u> <u>打电话</u> <u>找林总经理</u>。

总经理	今天	打电话	约见客户
康爱丽	明天	去上海	出差（chū chāi, to be on a business trip）
我们	周末	去饭馆	吃中国菜
我朋友	明年	要来北京	学习汉语

❺ <u>那</u> <u>你</u> <u>怎么</u> <u>不打</u> <u>我的手机</u>？

林总经理	不去	上海
你	不发	短信
小王	不知道	这件事
班长	不交（jiāo, to hand over）	作业

❻ <u>我</u> <u>觉得</u> <u>她应该会很喜欢的</u>。

我	康爱丽不会同意（tóngyì, to agree）这件事的
张经理	林经理会帮助他们公司的
爸爸	小明放假一定会回家的
卡尔	李明明可能不想去上海旅游
他	我们不应该大声（dà shēng, in a loud voice）说话
老师	他们可以下课以后听音乐
妈妈	女儿晚上应该早点儿回家

⑦ 你知道　她家　在哪儿　吗?

这个字	怎么读（dú, to read）
学生	几点下课
卡尔	什么时候回国
最近的地铁站	在哪儿

⑧ 咱们　周二下课后　走过去　就行。

你们	周五下班之前	做完调查（diàochá, to investigate）
我们	早上八点	到教室
张远	九月一日	去学校报到（bào dào, to register）
你	明天下午两点	来我的办公室
他们	下周一上午	把书还给图书馆

九 用下面的词语组成句子。
Make sentences with the following words and expressions.

① 细节　谈一谈　咱们　合作　的

② 和您　我　正好　见一面　想　也

③ 明天　忙　都　很　我　一天

④ 方便　时候　那　您　什么

⑤ 了　这样　那　定　就

⑥ 短信　一会儿　发　我　给　您

⑦ 吧　咱们　谈　见面

⑧ 了　客户　个　我　见　去

⑨ 呢　做过客　中国人　我　家里　还没去

⑩ 蛋糕　我　个　吧　订　给她　那

⑪ 在　她家　学校　旁边　就

➕ 用所给的词语完成对话。
Complete the dialogues with the given words.

① A：我去上海出差，你有什么事儿吗？

　　B：＿＿＿＿＿＿＿＿＿＿＿＿＿＿＿＿＿＿＿＿。（正好）

② A：我想知道林总经理的手机号码是多少。

　　B：＿＿＿＿＿＿＿＿＿＿＿＿＿＿＿＿＿＿＿＿。（可以）

③ A：这件衣服漂亮吗？

　　B：＿＿＿＿＿＿＿＿＿＿＿＿＿＿＿＿＿＿＿＿＿。（不过）

④ A：你知道小王家的地址吗？

　　B：＿＿＿＿＿＿＿＿＿＿＿＿＿＿＿＿＿＿＿＿＿。（就）

⑤ A：明天的聚会你女朋友参加吗？

　　B：＿＿＿＿＿＿＿＿＿＿＿＿＿＿＿＿＿＿＿＿＿。（会）

⑥ A：你写作业了吗？

　　B：＿＿＿＿＿＿＿＿＿＿＿＿＿＿＿＿＿＿＿＿。（还没……呢）

⑦ A：今天我收（shōu, to receive）到了很多礼物。

　　B：那你觉得＿＿＿＿＿＿＿＿＿＿＿＿＿＿＿＿＿＿？（最）

➕➖ 改错句。
Correct the following sentences.

① 我们进去教室吧。

② 卡尔回去德国了。

③ 他跑进来宿舍了。

④ 康爱丽走过去马路了。

⑤ 张远上来车了。

⑥ 明明下去楼了。

十二 用"来、去"填空。
Fill in the following blanks with "来" or "去".

① 卡尔不在家，见他的客户_____了。

② 这儿很远，你打车_____吧。

③ 卡尔在北京学汉语，他的妈妈到北京_____看他了。

④ 你怎么来了？明明给你送礼物_____了。

⑤ 外边很冷，进房间_____吧。

⑥ A: 爱丽，你什么时候过_____？我等你。

　　B: 我下午过_____。

⑦ 请举起手_____。

⑧ 明明回上海_____了，可是，她上海的朋友给她寄了一本书_____。

⑨ 他们还没出_____，我在门口等他们吧。

十三 阅读理解。
Reading comprehension.

　　卡尔是林总经理公司的客户，他们经常合作。星期一上午，卡尔给林总经理的办公室打电话，秘书说林总经理去上海出差了，后天回来，如果卡尔有急事儿，可以打林总经理的手机。卡尔说留言就可以。林总经理回来后，给卡尔回了电话。他们在电话中约好在一家咖啡厅见面，一起谈谈合作的细节。

判断正误：

Decide whether the following statements are true (√) or false (×)：

(　　　) ❶ 卡尔不认识林总经理。

(　　　) ❷ 卡尔不知道林总经理的手机号码。

(　　　) ❸ 林总经理星期二也不在办公室。

(　　　) ❹ 卡尔帮秘书给林总经理留言。

(　　　) ❺ 林总经理约卡尔在一家咖啡厅见面。

(　　　) ❻ 卡尔想和林总经理随便聊聊天儿。

十四 完成任务：请用课文中学过的词语和句子完成任务。

Complete the tasks: Please complete the tasks with the words and sentences you have learned in the texts.

1. 老师把自己的电话号码告诉学生，请学生下课后给老师打一个电话，问下次上课的时间、地点、学习内容等。

The teacher gives the students his telephone number and asks them to call him after class for the time, venue and content of the next class.

2. 给朋友打一个电话，商量周五下班以后去哪儿聚会，问清那个地方的详细地址以及怎么走。

Give your friend a call to discuss where to have a party after work on Friday and how to get there.

3. 从报纸或网络上找一个卖机票的广告，打电话咨询回国的机票价格、提前多长时间订票、怎么付钱、取票的方式等。

Find an advertisement on selling air tickets from the newspaper or the Internet. Make a phone call to ask about the price of the ticket to your country, how advanced the ticket is to be booked, and how to pay for and get the ticket, etc.

第九单元
UNIT **9**
谈论天气
Talking about the weather

明天天气怎么样
What will the weather be like tomorrow

课文 Text	题目 Title	注释 Notes
一	明天晴天 It will be sunny tomorrow	1. 动词"有"＋（数）量词"（一）点儿" The verb "有" ＋ quantifier / measure word "（一）点儿" 2. 传统节日：中秋节 A traditional festival: The Mid-Autumn Festival 3. 俗语"天公作美" The proverb "天公作美" 4. 介词"把"及"把"＋sb.＋V＋结果补语 The preposition "把" and "把" ＋ sb. ＋ V ＋ complement of result 5. 形容词"死" The adjective "死" 6. 连词"等" The conjunction "等" 7. 动词"完" The verb "完"
二	天气一天比一天冷 It's getting colder and colder	1. "一"＋量词＋"比"＋"一"＋量词 "一" ＋ measure word ＋ "比" ＋ "一" ＋ measure word 2. 动词"听说" The verb "听说" 3. "比"字句 The "比"-sentence 4. 比较句："A＋跟／和＋B＋一样（＋Adj／V）" The comparative sentence: "A＋跟／和＋B＋一样（＋Adj／V）"
三	北京的四季 Four seasons in Beijing	1. "越来越……" 2. 中国的长假制度 China's long-holiday system 3. 代词"各" The pronoun "各" 4. 温度的表达 The expressions of temperature

Míngtiān Qíngtiān
明天晴天
It will be sunny tomorrow

Kāng Àilì hé Kǎ'ěr zài qù jiàoshì de lùshang.

康爱丽和卡尔在去教室的路上。

Alice and Karl are on their way to the classroom.

Kāng Àilì: Kǎ'ěr, nǐ kàn tiānqì yùbào le ma? Míngtiān tiānqì zěnmeyàng?

● 康爱丽： 卡尔，你看天气预报了吗？明天天气怎么样？

Alice: Karl, have you watched the weather forecast? What will the weather be like tomorrow?

Kǎ'ěr: Kàn le. Míngtiān qíngtiān.

○ 卡尔： 看了。明天晴天。

Karl: Yes, I have. It will be sunny tomorrow.

Kāng Àilì: Yǒu fēng ma?

● 康爱丽： 有风吗？

Alice: Will it be windy?

Kǎ'ěr: Yǒu diǎnr fēng, búguò bú dà.

○ 卡尔： 有点儿风，不过不大。

Karl: A little bit, but not heavy.

Kāng Àilì: Tài hǎo le.
● 康爱丽： 太好了。
　　Alice:　　Great.

Kǎ'ěr:　Nǐ zěnme zhème guānxīn tiānqì?
○ 卡尔：　你怎么这么关心天气？
　　Karl:　　Why are you so concerned about the weather?

Kāng Àilì: Míngtiān shì Zhōngqiū Jié. Wǒmen gōngsī yào jǔbàn yì chǎng hùwài
● 康爱丽： 明天是中秋节。我们公司要举办一场户外

cùxiāo huódòng.
促销活动。
　　Alice:　　It is the Mid-Autumn Festival tomorrow. Our company will hold an outdoor
　　　　　　promoting activity.

Kǎ'ěr:　Zài nǎr?
○ 卡尔：　在哪儿？
　　Karl:　　Where?

Kāng Àilì: Wángfǔjǐng Dàjiē.
● 康爱丽： 王府井大街。
　　Alice:　　Wangfujing Street.

Kǎ'ěr:　Nǐ fàngxīn ba. Wǎngshang shuō wèilái jǐ tiān tiānqì dōu búcuò, wēndù
○ 卡尔：　你放心吧。网上说未来几天天气都不错，温度

bù gāo yě bù dī, méi shénme fēng, hěn shūfu.
不高也不低，没什么风，很舒服。
　　Karl:　　You can keep your mind at rest about the weather. The Internet says that it
　　　　　　will be sunny in the following days. The temperature is neither too high nor
　　　　　　too low and the wind is mild. It will be very pleasant.

Kāng Àilì: Tiāngōng zuòměi! Búguò, zuìjìn wǒmen gōngsī yǒu jǐ ge yuángōng xiū
● 康爱丽： 天公作美！不过，最近我们公司有几个员工休

niánjià, kě bǎ wǒ mángsǐ le.
年假，可把我忙死了。
　　Alice:　　Heaven is cooperative! But several staff of our company are on their annual
　　　　　　leave, and I am up to my ears these days.

Kǎ'ěr:　Míngtiān wǒ zhènghǎo yǒu kòngr, kěyǐ qù xiànchǎng bāng nǐ.
○ 卡尔：　明天我正好有空儿，可以去现场帮你。
　　Karl:　　I will be free tomorrow and I can help you on the site.

Kāng Àilì: Hǎo a! Xièxie nǐ! Děng huódòng wán le, wǒ qǐng nǐ chī fàn.

● 康爱丽： 好啊！谢谢你！等活动完了，我请你吃饭。

Alice: It's great, thank you. I will invite you to dinner after the activity.

Kǎ'ěr: Bié kèqi! Chī fàn jiù búyòng le.

○ 卡尔： 别客气！吃饭就不用了。

Karl: It's my pleasure, and you don't have to do it.

Kāng Àilì: Zhèyàng ba , wǒmen zhè cì huódòng yǒu yìxiē xiǎo lǐpǐn, wǒ sòng nǐ

● 康爱丽： 这样吧，我们这次活动有一些小礼品，我送你

yí jiàn ba.

一件吧。

Alice: Oh, we have some small gifts for this activity. I'll give you one.

生词　Shēngcí　New Words

1. 晴天	qíngtiān	N	sunny day
2. 天气	tiānqì	N	weather
3. 预报	yùbào	V	to forecast
4. 风	fēng	N	wind
5. 关心	guānxīn	V	to care, to concern
6. 举办	jǔbàn	V	to hold
7. 场	chǎng	M	*a measure word for activities*
8. 户外	hùwài	N	outdoor
9. 促销	cùxiāo	V	to promote the sales of goods
10. 活动	huódòng	N	activity
11. 放心	fàng xīn	V//O	to set one's mind at rest
12. 未来	wèilái	N	in the future
13. 温度	wēndù	N	temperature
14. 高	gāo	Adj	high
15. 低	dī	Adj	low

16. 舒服	shūfu	Adj	comfortable
17. 天公作美	tiāngōng zuòměi	IE	Heaven is cooperative
18. 员工	yuángōng	N	employee, staff
19. 休	xiū	V	to have one's vacation
20. 年假	niánjià	N	annual leave
21. 可	kě	Adv	really
22. 把	bǎ	Prep	*used to introduce "S + V + Comp" structure*
23. 死	sǐ	Adj	extremely, to death
24. 现场	xiànchǎng	N	scene
25. 完	wán	V	to finish
26. 一些	yìxiē	Q	some
27. 礼品	lǐpǐn	N	gift, present
28. 送	sòng	V	to send, to give

专有名词 Zhuānyǒu míngcí **Proper Nouns**

| 1. 中秋节 | Zhōngqiū Jié | the Mid-Autumn Festival |
| 2. 王府井大街 | Wángfǔjǐng Dàjiē | Wangfujing Street |

注释 Zhùshì **Notes**

1 **有点儿风，不过不大。** **A little bit (windy), but not heavy.**

"有（一）点儿"，这里是动词和量词的组合，即：动词"有"+（数）量词"（一）点儿"，不是我们在第1册第五单元课文三学过的副词。"有（一）点儿"后面带名词宾语，表示数量不大。例如：

"有（一）点儿" is a combination of a verb and a quantifier / measure word, i.e., verb (有) +

measure word "一点儿". It is not what we discussed in Text 3, Unit 5 of Book 1, in which it was used as an adverb. "有（一）点儿" is followed by a nominal object to indicate small amount. For example,

①杯子里有（一）点儿酒。
②这本书有（一）点儿意思。

2 明天是中秋节。It is the Mid-Autumn Festival tomorrow.

"中秋节"，农历（阴历）八月十五，是中国主要的传统节日之一。与春节（Chūn Jié）、端午节（Duānwǔ Jié）、清明节（Qīngmíng Jié）并称为中国的"四大传统节日"。人们把月圆当做团圆的象征，把农历八月十五作为亲人团聚的日子，因此，中秋节又被称为"团圆节"。中秋节人们最主要的活动就是赏月和吃月饼。除此之外，中国各地还有不同的习俗。2008 年开始，中国政府规定中秋节为国家法定节假日，放假一天。

Mid-Autumn Festival, falling on August 15th of the lunar calendar, is one of the four important traditional festivals in China, and the other three are the Spring Festival, the Dragon Boat Festival and the Tomb-Sweeping Day. Chinese people consider the round moon as the symbol of reunion and the lunar August 15th as the day for family reunion. Therefore, the Mid-Autumn Festival is also known as "the Festival of Reunion". On the Mid-Autumn Festival, the most important activity is to enjoy the wonderful view of the full moon and eat moon cakes. Besides, there are different customs in different areas of China. Since 2008, the Chinese government made the Mid-Autumn Festival as a national holiday, and people have a day off on that day.

3 天公作美！ Heaven is cooperative!

"天公作美"，俗语，表示事情的发展符合人们的愿望，正如人们想要的。这里的意思是：天气好，和我们希望的一样。常用在口语中。相反的意思是"天公不作美"。

"天公作美" is a proverb, indicating that something is developing as we hoped. Here it means that the weather is as good as we wish. It is often used in colloquial Chinese. The antonym is "天公不作美".

4 可把我忙死了。I am up to my ears these days.

"把"，介词，后面的动词是"忙、急、气（qì, to be angry）、累（lèi, to be tired）、乐（lè, to be happy）、美"等并加上表示结果的补语时，整个结构有致使的意思。常用在口语中。前面常加副词"可"，表示强调。基本结构："把" + sb. + V + 结果补语。例如：

The preposition "把" is followed by a verb and a complement of result. The verb is "忙", "急", "气", "累", "乐" or "美", etc. The basic structure "把" + sb. + V + complement of result means "to cause" and is often used in oral Chinese. It is often preceded by the adverb "可" to denote emphasis. For example,

	Adv（可）	Prep（把）	sb.	V	Complement of result
最近学习很忙，	可	把	我	累	死了。
最近工作很多，			他们	忙	
这么晚了她还没回家，			她父母	急	

5 **可把我忙死了。**　I am up to my ears these days.

"死"，这里是形容词，不表示结果，表示程度很高，达到极点。常放在动词或形容词的后面，并带上"了"。如"气死了、累死了、急死了"等。

The adjective "死" doesn't indicate a result, but an extremely high degree. It is often used after a verb or an adjective and followed by "了". For example, "气死了", "累死了", "急死了", etc.

6 **等活动完了，我请你吃饭。**　I will invite you to dinner after the activity.

"等"，连词，"等到"的意思。用于另一小句前，表示时间条件，可以带名词、动词、形容词、小句；后一小句常用"再、才、就"配合。例如：

The conjunction "等" means "to wait". It is used before another clause to indicate the condition of time and can be followed by a noun, verb, adjective or clause. The following clause is often used with "再", "才" or "就". For example,

① 我今天没空儿，这事儿等明天再说。

② 等他上完课，我们就走。

③ 别着急！等天晴了我们再出去玩儿。

④ 等我们到这儿，他已经走了。

7 **等活动完了，我请你吃饭。**　I will invite you to dinner after the activity.

"完"，动词，表示完成、完结。可以单独作谓语，也可以放在动词后作补语。动词的宾语常放在"完"后。例如：

"完", a verb, means "to finish or complete". It can serve as the predicate by itself or be put after a verb as a complement. The object of the verb is often put after "完". For example,

① 这件事情（shìqing, matter, business, thing）什么时候能完？

② 这本书我昨天就看完了。

③ 你做完作业了吗？

④ 上完课我想去买礼物。

Tiānqì Yì Tiān Bǐ Yì Tiān Lěng

天气一天比一天冷

It's getting colder and colder

Kǎ'ěr hé Kāng Àilì zài jiàoshì wàimian liáotiānr.

卡尔和康爱丽在教室外面聊天儿。

Karl and Alice are chatting outside the classroom.

Kāng Àilì: Tiānqì yì tiān bǐ yì tiān lěng, dōngtiān lái le.

● 康爱丽：天气一天比一天冷，冬天来了。

Alice: It's getting colder and colder. Winter is coming.

Kǎ'ěr: Shì a, jīntiān zhēn lěng! Shàngwán kè wǒ xiǎng qù mǎi yí jiàn yǔróngfú.

○ 卡尔： 是啊，今天真冷！上完课我想去买一件羽绒服。

Karl: Yes, it's so cold today. I want to buy a down coat after class.

Kāng Àilì: Gǎitiān wǒmen yìqǐ qù ba! Tīngshuō Běijīng de dōngtiān měi nián dōu

● 康爱丽：改天我们一起去吧！听说北京的冬天每年都

huì xià xuě.

会下雪。

Alice: Let's go together someday. It is said that it snows every winter in Beijing.

Kǎ'ěr: Tài hǎo le! Wǒ xǐhuan huábīng、huáxuě. Nǐ xǐhuan dōngtiān ma?

○ 卡尔： 太好了！我喜欢滑冰、滑雪。你喜欢冬天吗？

Karl: Wonderful! I like skating and skiing. Do you like winter?

Kāng Àilì: Wǒ bú tài xǐhuan dōngtiān, wǒ xǐhuan xiàtiān.

● 康爱丽：我不太喜欢冬天，我喜欢夏天。

Alice: I don't like winter. I like summer.

Kǎ'ěr: Wáng lǎoshī shuō, Běijīng de xiàtiān xiànzài bǐ yǐqián rè duō le, yòu mēn

○ 卡尔：王老师说，北京的夏天现在比以前热多了，又闷

yòu rè, hěn bù shūfu.

又热，很不舒服。

Karl: Mr. Wang says that summer in Beijing is much hotter than before. It's muggy and hot, making people very uncomfortable.

Kāng Àilì: Nà Běijīng nǎge jìjié zuì hǎo?

● 康爱丽：那北京哪个季节最好？

Alice: Which season is the best in Beijing?

Kǎ'ěr: Tīng wǒ de fǔdǎo lǎoshī shuō, Běijīng de qiūtiān zuì hǎo, bù lěng bú rè,

○ 卡尔：听我的辅导老师说，北京的秋天最好，不冷不热，

fēngjǐng yě hěn piàoliang. Shíyīyuè zuǒyòu, huì yǒu hěn duō rén qù

风景也很漂亮。十一月左右，会有很多人去

Xiāng Shān kàn hóngyè.

香山看红叶。

Karl: My supervisor says that autumn is the best season in Beijing, neither too cold nor too hot, and there are beautiful views. Around November, lots of people go to the Fragrant Mountain to appreciate the red leaves.

Kāng Àilì: Nà chūntiān ne? Chūntiān zěnmeyàng?

● 康爱丽：那春天呢？春天怎么样？

Alice: What about spring?

Kǎ'ěr: Chūntiān shùyè dōu lǜ le, huār yě kāi le, fēngjǐng gēn qiūtiān yíyàng

○ 卡尔：春天树叶都绿了，花儿也开了，风景跟秋天一样

piàoliang, jiù shì yǒushíhou fēng bǐjiào dà.

漂亮，就是有时候风比较大。

Karl: In spring, the leaves turn green and the flowers come out. It is as beautiful as autumn, but too windy sometimes.

生词　Shēngcí　**New Words**

1. 比	bǐ	Prep	*used for comparison*
2. 冷	lěng	Adj	cold
3. 冬天	dōngtiān	N	winter
4. 羽绒服	yǔróngfú	N	down coat
5. 改天	gǎitiān	Adv	someday
6. 听说	tīngshuō	V	to hear of
7. 雪	xuě	N	snow
8. 滑冰	huá bīng	V∥O	to skate
9. 滑雪	huá xuě	V∥O	to ski
10. 夏天	xiàtiān	N	summer
11. 热	rè	Adj	hot
12. 闷	mēn	Adj	stuffy, muggy
13. 季节	jìjié	N	season
14. 秋天	qiūtiān	N	autumn
15. 风景	fēngjǐng	N	landscape, scenery
16. 漂亮	piàoliang	Adj	beautiful
17. 十一月	shíyīyuè	N	November
18. 红叶	hóngyè	N	red leaf
19. 春天	chūntiān	N	spring
20. 树叶	shùyè	N	leaf
21. 绿	lǜ	Adj	green
22. 开	kāi	V	to blossom
23. 跟	gēn	Prep	with, and
24. 一样	yíyàng	Adj	same
25. 比较	bǐjiào	Adv	comparatively

专有名词	Zhuānyǒu Míngcí	**A Proper Noun**
香山	Xiāng Shān	a mountain in Beijing

注释　Zhùshì　**Notes**

1 **天气一天比一天冷。** **It's getting colder and colder.**

"一天比一天冷"，基本结构："一 ＋ 量词 ＋ 比 ＋ 一 ＋ 量词"，表示程度的累进。"比"的前后是"一"加量词的重复。例如：

This is a kind of "比"-sentence. The basic structure is "一 ＋ measure word ＋ 比 ＋ 一 ＋ measure word", indicating progression of degree. The same quantifier is used before and after "比". For example,

S	P			
	一 ＋ M	比	一 ＋ M	Predicative word
生活（shēnghuó, life）	一年		一年	好
天气	一天	比	一天	热。
他们	一个		一个	忙。

注意：这种结构中不能用"更"。例如：

Note: In this structure, "更" is not used. For example,

① 天气一天比一天更热。（×）
② 人们的生活一年比一年更好。（×）

2 **听说北京的冬天每年都会下雪。** **It is said that it snows every winter in Beijing.**

"听说"，动词，后面可以带主谓短语作宾语，否定式只能用"没（有）"。"听说"中间可以插入表示人的词语，即"听 sb. 说"。例如：

"听说", a verb, can be followed by a subject-predicate phrase as the object. The negative form is "没（有）". A word denoting people can be inserted between them, i.e. "听 sb. 说". For example,

① 我听说他去法国了。

② 卡尔听康爱丽说，李明明下周二过生日。

③ 你听谁说的？

④ 我听李明明说的。

⑤ 我们都知道了，你为什么没听说？

3 王老师说，北京的夏天现在比以前热多了。

Mr. Wang says that summer in Beijing is much hotter than before.

"比"字句，基本结构："A 比 B + Adj"。例如：

The basic structure of the "比" sentence is "A 比 B + Adj". For example,

A	比	B	Adj
北京		巴黎（Bālí, Paris）	热。
我	比	他	高。
她		我	大。

"比"字句的形容词后还可以加"多了、一点儿"等，构成："A 比 B + Adj + 多了/一点儿"。"多了"表示差别大，"一点儿"表示差别不大。例如：

Another form of the "比"-sentence is "A 比 B + Adj + 多了/一点儿". "多了" indicates a large difference, while "一点儿" indicates not much difference. For example,

A	比	B	Adj	多了/一点儿
北京的夏天		法国	热	多了。
她	比	我	大	一点儿。
我		他	高	多了。
现在	以前	暖和（nuǎnhuo, warm）	一点儿。

注意："比"字句中表示程度的加深，不能用"很"，可以用"更"，即："A 比 B + 更 + Adj"。表示 B 已经有了一定的程度，但 A 比 B 又高了一层。例如：

Note: "很" cannot be used in the "比"-sentence to indicate a higher degree, but "更" can. "A 比 B + 更 + Adj" indicates that B has reached a certain degree, but A is in a higher degree. For example,

A	比	B	更	Adj
这家饭馆	比	那家饭馆	更	贵。
今天		昨天		热。

4 （春天的）风景跟秋天一样漂亮，就是有时候风比较大。

It is as beautiful as autumn, but too windy sometimes.

比较句。基本结构："A + 跟/和 + B + 一样（+ Adj/ V）"。表示 A 在某一方面和 B 一样，比较的结果相同。A 和 B 可以是名词、代词，还可以是动词、形容词、动词短语或形容词短语。"一样"表示比较的结果，后面还可以有形容词或表示心理活动的动词及一些动词短语等。介词"跟/和"引进的 B 是比较句中作为参照的事物。"跟/和 + B + 一样"是"Adj/ V"的状语。例如：

This is a comparative sentence. The basic pattern "A + 跟/和 + B + 一样 (+ Adj / V)" indicates there is no difference between A and B in a certain aspect and the result of the comparison shows they are the same. A and B can be nouns, pronouns, verbs, adjectives, verbal phrases or adjective phrases. "一样" indicates the result of the comparison and can be followed by an adjective, a verb that indicates mental activity, or a verbal phrase. B introduced by the preposition "跟/和" serves as the reference. "跟/和 + B + 一样" is the adverbial of the adjective or the verb. For example,

A	跟/和	B	一样	Adj/V
卡尔的发音	跟/和	老师的发音	一样	好。
这件衣服		那件衣服		好看。
法语		德语（Déyǔ, German）		难。
他		我		大。
康爱丽		卡尔		喜欢吃中国菜。
读		写		难。
他来		我来		，都能帮你。

否定式为：（1）"A + 跟/和 + B + 不一样（+ Adj/V）"；（2）"A + 不跟/和 + B + 一样（+ Adj/V）"。例如：

The negative form is:（1）"A + 跟/和 + B + 一样（+ Adj / V）";（2）"A + 不跟/和 + B + 一样（+ Adj / V）". For example,

① 她不跟我一样高，跟李明明一样高。

② 在这句话里，"美丽（měilì, beautiful）"和"漂亮"的意思不一样。

③ 这双鞋（xié, shoes）6号，那双鞋7号。这双鞋跟那双鞋不一样大。/ 这双鞋的号码跟那双鞋不一样。

"跟……一样/不一样"还可以作定语。例如：

"跟……一样 / 不一样" can be used as an attributive. For example,

④ 我有一条跟你的这条颜色（yánsè, color）一样的裙子。

⑤ 我买了一辆跟他的那辆不一样的车。

⑥ 请问，这儿有跟这支（zhī, a measure word）一样的笔吗？

Běijīng de Sìjì

北京的四季

Four seasons in Beijing

Kèwén Sān
课文三
Text 3

Běijīng zài Zhōngguó de běifāng, yì nián yǒu chūn、xià、qiū、dōng sì ge jìjié.
北京在中国的北方，一年有春、夏、秋、冬四个季节。
Xiàtiān hé dōngtiān bǐjiào cháng, chūntiān hé qiūtiān bǐjiào duǎn.
夏天和冬天比较长，春天和秋天比较短。

Beijing lies in the north of China. It has four seasons in a year: spring, summer, autumn and winter. Summer and winter are long, and spring and autumn are short.

Chūntiān hěn nuǎnhuo, fēngjǐng yě hěn měi, búguò yǒudiǎnr gānzào. Yǐqián,
春天很暖和，风景也很美，不过有点儿干燥。以前，
fēngshā bǐjiào dà, xiànzài kōngqì de zhìliàng yuè lái yuè hǎo le.
风沙比较大，现在空气的质量越来越好了。

In spring, the weather is mild and the views are beautiful, but it is a little bit dry. In the past, it was windy and dusty. But these years, the air quality is getting better and better.

Xiàtiān yǔshuǐ bǐjiào duō, báitiān de píngjūn wēndù zài sānshí dù zuǒyòu.
夏天雨水比较多，白天的平均温度在三十度左右。

In summer, it rains a lot. The average temperature in the daytime is around 30 degrees Celsius.

Qiūtiān hěn liángkuai, shì yì nián zhōng zuì hǎo de jìjié, yě shì lǚyóu wàngjì.

秋天很凉快，是一年中最好的季节，也是旅游旺季。

Shí-Yī huángjīnzhōu huì yǒu chéng qiān shàng wàn de yóukè lái Běijīng, gègè lǚyóu

十一黄金周会有成千上万的游客来北京，各个旅游

jǐngdiǎn de rén dōu hěn duō.

景点的人都很多。

In autumn, it is very cool. It is the best season of the year as well as the tourist peak season. During the Golden Week of National Day, tens of thousands of people visit Beijing. Each scenic spot is crowded with people.

Dōngtiān hěn lěng, yǒushí zuì dī wēndù huì dádào língxià shíjǐ dù. Rénmen

冬天很冷，有时最低温度会达到零下十几度。人们

dōu yào chuān hěn hòu de yǔróngfú. Nǐmen guójiā ne?

都要穿很厚的羽绒服。你们国家呢？

In winter, it is very cold, with the lowest temperature of more than ten degrees below zero. People wear very thick down coats. What about your country?

生词　Shēngcí　**New Words**

1. 四季	sìjì	N	four seasons
2. 北方	běifāng	N	the north
3. 短	duǎn	Adj	short
4. 暖和	nuǎnhuo	Adj	warm
5. 美	měi	Adj	beautiful
6. 干燥	gānzào	Adj	dry
7. 风沙	fēngshā	N	sand blown by the wind, sandstorm
8. 空气	kōngqì	N	air
9. 质量	zhìliàng	N	quality
10. 越来越	yuè lái yuè		more and more
11. 雨水	yǔshuǐ	N	rainwater
12. 白天	báitiān	N	daytime

13. 平均	píngjūn	Adj	average
14. 度	dù	N	degree
15. 凉快	liángkuai	Adj	cool
16. 中	zhōng	N	during
17. 旅游	lǚyóu	V	to travel
18. 旺季	wàngjì	N	busy season
19. 十一	Shí-Yī	N	National Day
20. 黄金周	huángjīnzhōu	N	golden week
21. 成千上万	chéng qiān shàng wàn		thousands of
22. 游客	yóukè	N	tourist
23. 各个	gègè	Pr	each, every
各	gè	Pr	each, every
24. 景点	jǐngdiǎn	N	scenic spot
25. 达到	dádào	V	to reach
26. 零下	língxià	N	below zero
27. 人们	rénmen	N	people
28. 国家	guójiā	N	country

注释 Zhùshì **Notes**

1 现在空气的质量越来越好了。But these years, the air quality is getting better and better.

"越来越"，表示程度随着时间而发展。可以作状语，放在形容词和表示心理活动的动词前面。例如：

"越来越" indicates the degree grows as time goes on. It can be used as an adverbial and placed before an adjective or a verb indicating mental activity. For example,

① 天气越来越冷。

② 他的汉语水平越来越高。

③ 小王的脸越来越红。

④ 他们越来越爱这个国家。

注意："越来越"应该放在它所修饰的形容词或动词的前面，不能放在主语前。例如：

Note: "越来越" is used before the adjective or verb it modifies, not the subject. For example,

⑤ 他越来越喜欢汉语了。（ √ ）

⑥ 越来越他喜欢汉语了。（ × ）

2 **十一黄金周会有成千上万的游客来北京。**

During the Golden Week of National Day, tens of thousands of people visit Beijing.

中国的长假制度。"黄金周"，又称"长假"。中国政府规定，国庆节、春节各放假3天，加上前后的两个周末，可以连续休假7天。长假的制定带动了"假日经济"的发展。7天长假是旅游、交通和商业的集中时段，给商家带来了巨大的商机，媒体将它们称为"黄金周"。除了7天长假，中国政府还规定元旦、清明节、劳动节、端午节、中秋节各放假1天，加上前后的周末，可以连续休息3天，又称"小长假"。

China's long-holiday system. "The Golden Week" is also known as the "Long Holiday". The Chinese government stipulates that on the National Day and the Spring Festival, people have seven days off in a row, i.e. three days off coupled with the two weekends before and after them. The stipulation of the long holidays brings along the development of the "Holiday Economy". These seven-day holidays are the peaks of tourism, transportation and business and bring vast business opportunities, therefore are referred to as the "Golden Week" by the media. Besides the seven-day holidays, the Chinese government also stipulates that on the New Year, the Tomb-Sweeping Day, the Labor Day, the Dragon Boat Festival and the Mid-Autumn Festival, people have three days off in a row, i.e., a day off coupled with the weekend before or after it. They are referred to as the "Small Long Holiday".

3 **各个旅游景点的人都很多。** Each scenic spot is crowded with people.

"各"，代词，表示全体中的所有个体。这里的"各个"也是代词，表示"每个、所有的那些个"。"各"可以单用，也可以用在名词或量词前。

"各", a pronoun, indicates all the individuals of a whole. "各个", a pronoun, means "each". It can be used either by itself or before a noun or a measure word.

可以和"各"连用的名词限于人、机构、组织、单位等，如"各国、各地、各部门（bùmén, department）、各单位（dānwèi, unit）、各公司、各学校、各班（bān, class）、各人"等。

The nouns that can be used together with "各" are only those that indicate people, institutions, organizations, or units, etc, for example, "各国", "各地", "各部门", "各单位", "各公司", "各学校", "各班", and "各人", etc.

能与"各"连用的量词也是有限的，主要有"个、位、门、项（xiàng）、级（jí）、类（lèi）、种（zhǒng）、界（jiè）"等。

There are not many measure words that can be used together with "各", which mainly include "个", "位", "门", "项", "级", "类", "种", and "界", etc.

4 有时最低温度会达到零下十几度。

… with the lowest temperature of more than ten degrees below zero.

温度的表达。中国一般用摄氏度来表示温度，符号是℃，口语中，一般读做"度"，如30℃读做"30度"。摄氏度与华氏度（℉）的换算关系如下：

华氏度 = 32 + 摄氏度 ×1.8

摄氏度 =（华氏度 − 32）÷1.8

Expressions for temperature. In China, degree Celsius is usually used to denote temperature. The symbol is ℃. In oral Chinese, we usually read it as "度". For example, 30℃ is read as "30度". The conversion between the degree Celsius and degree Fahrenheit is as follows:

Degree Fahrenheit = 32 + Degree Celsius ×1.8

Degree Celsius = (Degree Fahrenheit −32) ÷1.8

摄氏度（Shèshìdù）℃ Degree Celsius	华氏度（Huáshìdù）℉ Degree Fahrenheit
37℃	98.6℉
0℃	32℉
100℃	212℉

练习　Liànxí　Exercises

一 跟读生词，注意发音和声调。
Read the new words after the teacher and pay attention to your pronunciation and tones.

二 跟读课文，注意语音语调。
Read the texts after the teacher and pay attention to your pronunciation and intonation.

三 学生分组，分角色朗读课文一、二；分段朗读课文三。
Divide the students into groups and read Texts 1 & 2 in roles, Text 3 paragraph by paragraph in turns.

四 学生分组，不看书，分角色表演课文一、二。
Divide the students into groups and play the roles in Texts 1 & 2 without referring to the book.

五 角色扮演。（提示：角色可以互换。）
Role playing. (Note: the roles can be exchanged.)

1. 两个学生一组，用下面的生词和句型分别介绍自己的国家或自己所在城市的天气。
Students work in pairs to talk about the weather in their countries or cities with the following new words and sentence patterns.

四季　　春天　　夏天　　秋天　　冬天　　暖和　　干燥　　凉快　　冷　　热
刮风　　下雨　　下雪　　温度　　越来越　　一天比一天
不Adj$_1$，也不Adj$_2$

2. 两个学生一组，比较一下你们国家的天气和中国天气的差别。
Students work in pairs to compare the differences between the weather in their countries and that in China.

六 复述课文一和课文二。
Retell Texts 1 & 2.

七 看图回答问题。
Answer the questions according to the pictures.

1. 下面的图分别是哪个季节？ Which season does the picture show?

(   )   (   )

(   )   (   )

2. 今天天气怎么样？ What's the weather like today?

(   )   (   )   (   )

(   )   (   )   (   )

3. 他们在做什么？ What are they doing?

（　　） （　　） （　　）

（　　） （　　） （　　）

八 替换练习。
Substitution drills.

① 春天的风景　比　秋天　漂亮。

昨天的风	今天的风	大
冬天的气温（qìwēn, air temperature）	夏天的气温	低
我学汉语的时间	她学汉语的时间	长
这种苹果	那种苹果	甜
我的个子 (gèzi, height, stature)	他的个子	高

② 北京的夏天　比　法国　热　多了。

我们的教室	他们的教室	干净	多了
他	他哥哥	聪明 (cōngming, clever)	多了
这里的风景	那里的风景	漂亮	多了
今天的汉字	昨天的汉字	多	10个
我们班的学生	他们班的学生	少	3个
坐飞机	坐火车	快	8个小时

③ 天气　一天　比　一天　冷。

学汉语的人	一年	一年	多
我们的生活	一天	一天	好
他们的收入（shōurù, income）	一个月	一个月	少
来北京旅游的人	一年	一年	多
他的个子	一天	一天	高

④ 春天的风景　跟　秋天　一样　漂亮。

北京的天气	上海的天气	热
我的房间	他的房间	舒服
中国菜	西班牙（Xībānyá, Spain）菜	好吃
这个星期的工作	上个星期的工作	多

⑤ 气温　越来越　高。

这个孩子	不听话（tīng huà, to be obedient）
这里的空气质量	好
学习	容易
他的女朋友	喜欢看电影
明明	害怕（hài pà, to be scared）

九 用下面的词语组成句子。
Make sentences with the following words and expressions.

① 这么　怎么　你　天气　关心

② 有　我们　最近　公司　休年假　几个　员工

③ 正好　明天　空儿　有　我

④ 送　小　一件　我　你　礼品

⑤ 去　羽绒服　上完课　想　我　买　一件

⑥ 我们　吧　一起　改天　去

⑦ 不　冬天　我　喜欢　太

⑧ 去香山　会　十一月左右　很多人　有　看红叶

⑨ 成千上万　有　的　黄金周　来北京　游客　会

⑩ 很多　景点　各个　旅游　人　都　的

✚ 模仿造句。
Make sentences following the examples.

1. 北京的秋天<u>不冷也不热</u>，很舒服。

① 今天的温度_____。

② 这些东西的价格（jiàgé, price）_____。

③ 这条裙子_____。

④ 这双鞋_____。

⑤ 我们的教室_____。

2. 一个人做这么多工作，<u>可把我忙死了</u>。

① 走了这么长时间的路，可把我_____。

② 他的孩子病了，可把他_____。

③ 今天40度，没有空调（kōngtiáo, air-conditioner），可把我们_____。

④ 孩子很晚还没有回来，可把父母_____。

⑤ 这几天只睡了五个小时，可把我_____。

3. 等活动完了，我把我们公司的礼品送给你。

① _____，我们一起去旅游。

② _____，我带你去长城玩儿。

③ _____，我们去那儿买东西。

④ _____，我再给你打电话。

4. 听我的辅导老师说，秋天是最漂亮的季节。

① _____，明天要下雨。

② _____，他学习特别认真。

③ _____，滑雪特别有意思。

④ _____，他的病很快就会好。

5. 秋天是一年中最好的季节。

① 他是_____最聪明的学生。

② 北京是_____人最多的城市（chéngshì, city）。

③ 长城是_____最有名（yǒumíng, famous）的景点。

④ 中秋节是_____我最喜欢的节日。

十一 选词填空。
Fill in the blanks with the correct words.

正好	听说	旅游	关心	促销
现场	达到	平均	改天	放心

① 北京人每个月的（　　　　）工资（gōngzī, salary）是3000块左右。

② 父母非常（　　　　）孩子的身体。

③ 周末的时候，有的超市有（　　　　）活动。

④ 我（　　　）他下个月就要结婚了。

⑤ 对不起，今天我有点儿事儿，（　　　）一定陪（péi, to accompany）你吃饭。

⑥ 假期的时候他去外地（wàidì, other places）（　　　）了。

⑦ 这些东西一共35块，你的钱（　　　）。

⑧ 我没有去（　　　），我是通过电视看的比赛（bǐsài, game）。

⑨ 他的要求（yāoqiú, deman）很高，我们很难（　　　）。

⑩ 你（　　　）吧，我一到北京就给你打电话。

十二 用所给词语完成对话。

Complete the dialogues with the given words or expressions.

① A：北京的秋天天气怎么样？

　　B：_____。（不Adj$_1$，也不Adj$_2$）

② A：你们两人谁大？

　　B：_____。（比）

③ A：明天考试，今天你做什么？

　　B：_____。（得+V）

④ A：这个公司的产品质量怎么样？

　　B：_____。（比较+Adj）

⑤ A：你什么时候学会用筷子（kuàizi, chopsticks）的？

　　B：_____。（……以后）

十三 改写句子。

Rewrite the sentences.

1. 跟……一样/不一样

Example：我学汉语，他也学汉语。 ——→ 我跟他学的一样。

① 这瓶酒500元，那瓶酒也是500元。 ——→

② 我的电脑是这个牌子的，他的电脑也是这个牌子的。 ——→

③ 今天北京 30 度，上海也 30 度。——→

④ 我们去了香山，他们也去了香山。——→

⑤ 卡尔住在学校的公寓里，康爱丽住在外边。——→

⑥ 小王口语考试的成绩（chéngjì, result）是 90 分，小张是 85 分。——→

⑦ 明明的裙子是黑的，爱丽的是灰的。——→

2. 跟……一样/不一样 + Adj / V

Example：我 35 岁，卡尔也是 35 岁。——→ 我跟卡尔一样大。

① 我吃素，他也吃素。——→

② 沃尔玛的香蕉 3 块钱一斤，家乐福的香蕉也是 3 块钱一斤。——→

③ 这件红色（hóngsè, red）的羽绒服 1000 元，那条蓝色（lánsè, blue）的裤子也是 1000 元。——→

④ 这个国家没有冬天，那个国家也没有冬天。——→

⑤ 他想当经理，明明也想当经理。——→

⑥ 卡尔的行李 20 公斤，张远的行李 25 公斤。——→

⑦ 我们班 10 个学生，他们班 12 个学生。——→

十四 阅读理解。

Reading comprehension.

现在播报未来几天的天气情况。由于受冷空气的影响，未来几天，中国北方城市将会迎来入冬以来第一次大范围的降温，部分地区有小雪。南方的雨将会持续到这个周末，部分地区有暴雨。首都北京的气温在零下 2 度到 5 度之间，有 4 级左右大风，如果出门，最好穿上厚衣服。

生词 Shēngcí New Words

1. 播报	bōbào	V	to broadcast
2. 情况	qíngkuàng	N	situation, condition
3. 由于	yóuyú	Prep	owing to, due to
4. 受	shòu	V	to be affected by, to be subjected to
5. 影响	yǐngxiǎng	N	influence
6. 将	jiāng	Adv	be going to, be about to
7. 迎来	yínglái	V	to meet, to receive, to usher in
8. 入冬	rù dōng		to start the winter
9. 以来	yǐlái	N	since
10. 范围	fànwéi	N	limits, scope
11. 降温	jiàng wēn	V//O	to drop in temperature
12. 部分	bùfen	N	part, section
13. 地区	dìqū	N	area
14. 持续	chíxù	V	to last, to sustain
15. 首都	shǒudū	N	capital
16. 级	jí	N	scale, level, rank
17. 出门	chū mén	V//O	to go out
18. 最好	zuìhǎo	Adv	had better

判断正误：

Decide whether the following statements are true (√) or false (×)：

(   ) ① 未来几天中国北方的天气将越来越暖和。

114

(　) ② 北京的最高温度是 5 度。

(　) ③ 现在是冬天。

(　) ④ 南方有的地方有小雪。

(　) ⑤ 天气很冷，所以不要出门。

十五 完成任务：请用课文中学过的词语和句子完成任务。
Complete the tasks: Please complete the tasks with the words and sentences you have learned in the texts.

---

1. 请下课回去以后听一下第二天的天气预报，在第二天的课堂上告诉老师和同学你听到的天气情况。
   Please watch the weather forecast for tomorrow after school, and present the weather information to your teacher and classmates in class tomorrow.

2. 分组讨论：
   Group discussions:
   （1）现在，全球气候变暖已经成为一个非常严重的问题，你觉得你们国家在哪些方面受到了这一影响？现在和10年前比，有什么变化？
   Nowadays, global warming has become a very serious problem. Do you feel your country has been affected by it? What changes have taken place since 10 years ago?
   （2）你觉得气候变暖对我们未来的生活有什么影响？你认为有什么办法能解决这个问题？
   How do you feel the global warming will affect our lives in the future? In your opinion, how can we solve this problem?

   每个小组讨论结束以后，请选一位同学代表本组向全班介绍讨论的结果。
   After the discussion, select a student to give a presentation of the result of the discussion in class on behalf of your group.

你喜欢什么运动
What sports do you like

课文 Text	题目 Title	注释 Notes
一	周末你打算做什么 What are you going to do this weekend	1. 动词兼名词"打算" The verb and noun "打算" 2. "一 A 就 B" 3. 情态补语 The modal complement 4. "一 ＋ V ＋ 就（是）＋ Q" 5. "除了……以外／之外／外，还／也……"
二	您是什么时候开始打球的 When did you begin to play golf	1. "您几位"询问人数 "您几位" is used to inquire the number of people 2. 介词"为" The preposition "为" 3. 动量词 The measure words for actions 4. 疑问代词"如何" The interrogative pronoun "如何" 5. 代词"哪里"表示谦虚 The pronoun "哪里" indicates one's modesty 6. 习惯用语"看我的" The idiom "看我的" 7. "是……的"句 The "是……的" sentence 8. "越 A 越 B" 9. 连词"而且" The conjunction "而且" 10. 介词"通过" The preposition "通过" 11. 副词"再"（复习） The adverb "再" (Review) 12. 高尔夫球运动常用术语 Frequently used golf terms

| 三 | 怀柔拓展训练行程安排
Schedule of the field training in Huairou | 能愿动词"得（dé）"
The optative verb "得（dé）" |

Zhōumò Nǐ Dǎsuàn Zuò Shénme

周末你打算做什么

What are you going to do this weekend

Kǎ'ěr hé Zhāng Yuǎn zài liáotiānr.

卡尔和张远在聊天儿。

Karl and Zhang Yuan are chatting.

Zhāng Yuǎn: Kǎ'ěr, zhōumò nǐ dǎsuàn zuò shénme?

● 张远： 卡尔，周末你打算做什么？

Zhang Yuan: Karl, what are you going to do this weekend?

Kǎ'ěr: Wǒ xiǎng qù jiànshēnfáng.

○ 卡尔： 我想去健身房。

Karl: I want to go to the gymnasium.

Zhāng Yuǎn: Nǐ chángcháng jiànshēn ma?

● 张远： 你常常健身吗？

Zhang Yuan: Do you often go there?

Kǎ'ěr: Duì, wǒ hěn xǐhuan yùndòng, yì yǒu shíjiān wǒ jiù qù jiànshēnfáng

○ 卡尔： 对，我很喜欢运动，一有时间我就去健身房

duànliàn shēntǐ.

锻炼身体。

Karl: Yes, I like sports very much, and I go to the gymnasium to do exercises as long as I have time.

Zhāng Yuǎn: Nǐ xǐhuan shénme yùndòng?

● 张远： 你喜欢什么运动？

Zhang Yuan: What sports do you like?

Kǎ'ěr: Wǒ zuì xǐhuan yóuyǒng, yǒushíhou yě dǎda lánqiú、tīti zúqiú.

○ 卡尔： 我最喜欢游泳，有时候也打打篮球、踢踢足球。

Karl: I like swimming the best. But I also play basketball and football sometimes.

Zhāng Yuǎn: Nǐ yóuyǒng yóu de zěnmeyàng?

● 张远： 你游泳游得怎么样？

Zhang Yuan: Are you a good swimmer?

Kǎ'ěr: Wǒ yóu de búcuò, yí cì néng yóu bābǎi mǐ. Nǐ ne?

○ 卡尔： 我游得不错，一次能游八百米。你呢？

Karl: Yes, I can swim 800 meters at one time. What about you?

Zhāng Yuǎn: Zhēn xiànmù nǐ! Wǒ shì ge hànyāzi!

● 张远： 真羡慕你！我是个旱鸭子！

Zhang Yuan: I envy you so much. I am a landlubber!

Kǎ'ěr: Nà nǐ xǐhuan shénme yùndòng?

○ 卡尔： 那你喜欢什么运动？

Karl: Then what sports do you like?

Zhāng Yuǎn: Wǒ zhǐ xǐhuan kàn biéren yùndòng, bù xǐhuan zìjǐ yùndòng. Diànshì

● 张远： 我只喜欢看别人运动，不喜欢自己运动。电视

shang yì yǒu tǐyù bǐsài, wǒ jiù zuò zài shāfā shang kàn, yí kàn jiù shì

上一有体育比赛，我就坐在沙发上看，一看就是

jǐ ge zhōngtóu.

几个钟头。

Zhang Yuan: I like watching sports, but not doing sports myself. Once there is a game on TV, I would sit on the couch and watch it for a couple of hours.

Kǎ'ěr: Chúle kàn diànshì yǐwài, nǐ hái yǒu shénme àihào?

○ 卡尔： 除了看电视以外，你还有什么爱好？

Karl: Besides watching TV, what other hobbies do you have?

Zhāng Yuǎn: Wǒ hái xǐhuan kàn diànyǐng、tīng yīnyuè. Nǐ ne?

● 张远： 我还喜欢看电影、听音乐。你呢？

Zhang Yuan: I like seeing movies and listening to the music. And you?

Kǎ'ěr: Wǒ de àihào shì kàn shū、lǚxíng.
○ 卡尔：   我的爱好是看书、旅行。
Karl: I like reading and traveling.

	生词	Shēngcí	New Words	
1.	打算	dǎsuàn	V/N	to plan; plan
2.	健身房	jiànshēnfáng	N	gymnasium
3.	健身	jiànshēn	V	to keep fit
4.	运动	yùndòng	V/N	to exercise; sport
5.	锻炼	duànliàn	V	to have exercises
6.	身体	shēntǐ	N	body
7.	游泳	yóuyǒng	V	to swim
8.	打	dǎ	V	to play
9.	篮球	lánqiú	N	basketball
10.	踢	tī	V	to kick, to play
11.	足球	zúqiú	N	football
12.	米	mǐ	M	meter
13.	羡慕	xiànmù	V	to envy
14.	旱鸭子	hànyāzi	N	landlubber
15.	只	zhǐ	Adv	only, just
16.	别人	biéren	Pr	other people
17.	电视	diànshì	N	television
18.	体育	tǐyù	N	sports
19.	比赛	bǐsài	N	game, match
20.	沙发	shāfā	N	sofa
21.	钟头	zhōngtóu	N	hour
22.	除了	chúle	Prep	except (for)

23.	以外	yǐwài	N	beyond, outside
24.	爱好	àihào	N	hobby
25.	电影	diànyǐng	N	movie
26.	音乐	yīnyuè	N	music
27.	旅行	lǚxíng	V	to travel, to tour

注释　Zhùshì　**Notes**

1 周末你打算做什么？ **What are you going to do this weekend?**

"打算"，动词，"事先考虑、计划"的意思。不能带名词宾语，要带动词和小句宾语，可以带补语。例如：

The verb "打算" means to "consider or plan in advance". Its object is not a noun, but a verb or a clause. It can be followed by a complement. For example,

① 国庆长假你打算去哪儿旅行？

② 他们打算怎么去上海？

③ 我打算明年去法国留学（liú xué, to study abroad）。

"打算"还是名词，表示事先的想法、计划。可以作主语和宾语。例如：

"打算" is also a noun, indicating the original thought or plan. It can serve as a subject or an object. For example,

④ 这个周末你有什么打算？

⑤ 快放假了，说说你的打算。

2 一有时间我就去健身房锻炼身体。

I go to the gymnasium to do exercises as long as I have time.

"一 A 就 B"，表示 A、B 两个动作或情况紧接着发生。"就"字前后的两个动词不一样，主语可以相同，也可以不同。例如：

"一 A 就 B" indicates the two actions or states A and B happen one after another. The verbs before and after "就" are not the same, but the subject of each verb can be either the same or different. For example,

① 这句话他们一学就会。

② 她一有空儿就上网。

③ 老师一解释（jiěshì, to explain）我就懂了。

④ 我们一到北京，天就热了。

⑤ 电视上一有体育比赛，我就坐在沙发上看。

3 **张远：你游泳游得怎么样？卡尔：我游得不错。**

Zhang Yuan: Are you a good swimmer? Karl: Yes.

情态补语。"游得不错"，谓语动词"游"后面带的是情态补语"不错"。情态补语是补充、说明以及描写动作行为的情况、状态、结果的。基本结构：动词／形容词＋"得"＋情态补语。可以作情态补语的词语有形容词短语、动词短语、主谓短语、名词短语等。例如：

It is a modal complement. In "游得不错", the predicate verb "游" is followed by the modal complement "不错". The modal complement is used to complement, explain or describe the situation, state or result of the action. Its basic pattern is: Verb / Adjective + "得" + modal complement. The words and phrases that serve as modal complements include adjective ones, verbal ones, subject-predicate ones, and nominal ones, etc. For example,

① 康爱丽汉语说得很流利（liúlì, fluent）。

② 王老师看书看得忘了吃饭。

③ 她高兴得跳了起来（qǐlai, *used after a verb to indicate an upward movement*）。

④ 卡尔急得脸都红了。

情态补语的肯定形式、否定形式、疑问形式分别是：

The affirmative, negative, and interrogative forms of a modal complement are:

肯定式	Affirmative sentence	他游泳游得不错。
否定式	Negative sentence	他游泳游得不好。
疑问式	Interrogative sentence	他游泳游得好不好 / 好吗 / 怎么样？

动宾结构或动宾式离合词带情态补语时，要重复动词。例如：

If the predicate-object structure or the verb-object compound is followed by a modal complement, the verb is repeated. For example,

⑤ 妈妈扫地（sǎo dì, to sweep the floor）扫得很干净。

⑥ 李明明唱歌唱得很好听。

"越来越……"可以用在情态补语中，放在"得"的后面。例如：

"越来越……" is used as a modal complement after "得". For example,

⑦ 他的汉语说得越来越好。

⑧ 爸爸的脾气（píqi, temper）变（biàn, to change）得越来越坏。

4 电视上一有体育比赛，我就坐在沙发上看，一看就是几个钟头。

Once there is a game on TV, I would sit on the couch and watch it for a couple of hours.

"一 + 动词 + 就（是）+ 数量词"，常用格式，这里表示说话人认为数量多。有时句子中没有数量词，但还是含有数量的意思。例如：

The frequently used pattern "一 + verb + 就（是）+ quantifier" indicates the speaker thinks the amount is large. Sometimes, there is not a quantifier in a sentence, but it still indicates amount. For example,

① 卡尔一说就是二十分钟。

② 他一住就是三个月。

③ 她一唱就没完没了 (méi wán méi liǎo, not stop)。

5 除了看电视以外，你还有什么爱好？

Besides watching TV, what other hobbies do you have?

"除了……以外 / 之外 / 外，还 / 也……"，表示所说的不计算在内，后一分句配合使用的是"还、也"，表示在前一分句"除了"的宾语所表示的已知的人或事物之外，还有别的。"除了"后面的宾语可以是代词、名词、动词、形容词、主谓短语等。"除"和"除了"的意思基本一样，但"除了"更常用。例如：

"除了……以外 / 之外 / 外，还 / 也……" indicates what is said is not included. "还" or "也" used in the following clause indicates that there are other things besides the people or thing referred to by the object of "除了" in the preceding clause. The object used after "除了" can be a pronoun, a noun, a verb, an adjective, or a subject-predicate phrase, etc. "除" and "除了" are basically the same in meaning, but, "除了" is used more often. For example,

① 除了学习以外，我们还要在中国工作。

② 除了苹果，你还买了什么？

③ 周末晚上我们除了看电影、逛街（guàng jiē, to go window-shopping）外，还去了酒吧（jiǔbā, bar）。

④ 除了康爱丽之外，卡尔也参加了这次研讨会。

Nín Shì Shénme Shíhou Kāishǐ Dǎ Qiú de

您是什么时候开始打球的
When did you begin to play golf

Kǎ'ěr qǐng tā de kèhù Lín jīnglǐ yìqǐ qù dǎ gāo'ěrfūqiú.

卡尔请他的客户林经理一起去打高尔夫球。

Karl invites Manager Lin, his client, to play golf together.

Fúwùyuán: Xiānsheng，huānyíng nín láidào wǒmen jùlèbù! Nín yùyuēle ma?

● 服务员：   先生，欢迎您来到我们俱乐部！您预约了吗？

Service person: Sir, welcome to our club. Have you made a reservation?

Kǎ'ěr: Yùyuē le. Zhè shì wǒ de huìyuánkǎ.

○ 卡尔：   预约了。这是我的会员卡。

Karl: Yes, this is my membership card.

Fúwùyuán: Xièxie! Nín jǐ wèi yìqǐ dǎ qiú?

● 服务员：   谢谢！您几位一起打球？

Service person: Thank you! How many of you are going to play golf?

Kǎ'ěr: Liǎng wèi.

○ 卡尔：   两位。

Karl: Two.

	Fúwùyuán:	Hǎo de. Xiànzài ānpái qiútóng wèi nín fúwù.
●	服务员:	好的。现在安排球童为您服务。
	Service person:	OK. I will send a caddy to help you.

	Qiútóng:	Xiānsheng，qǐng nín kàn yíxià，zhè shì nín de qiúbāo ma?
○	球童:	先生，请您看一下，这是您的球包吗？
	Caddy:	Sir, please have a look, is this your golf bag?

	Kǎ'ěr:	Shì.
●	卡尔:	是。
	Karl:	Yes.

Tāmen zǒuxiàng chǎngdì.
他们走向场地。
They are walking to the golf course.

	Lín jīnglǐ:	Zhè jiā jùlèbù wǒ háishi dì yī cì lái. Chǎngdì búcuò!
○	林经理:	这家俱乐部我还是第一次来。场地不错！
	Manager Lin:	It's my first time to come to this club. A nice course!

	Kǎ'ěr:	Shì a! Zhèr shì shíbā dòng qīshí'èr gān de guójì biāozhǔn
●	卡尔:	是啊！这儿是 18 洞 72 杆的国际标准
		qiúchǎng，shǔyú shāndìxíng qiúchǎng.
		球场，属于山地型球场。
	Karl:	Yes. This is the 18-hole 72-club international standard golf course, a kind of hilly course.

	Lín jīnglǐ:	Zhèr de liànxíchǎng zěnmeyàng?
○	林经理:	这儿的练习场怎么样？
	Manager Lin:	How about the driving range here?

	Kǎ'ěr:	Hái kěyǐ，tuī gān guǒlǐng、qiē gān guǒlǐng、liànxí shākēng dōu
●	卡尔:	还可以，推杆果岭、切杆果岭、练习沙坑都
		yǒu，dōu búcuò.
		有，都不错。
	Karl:	It's nice. Putting green, pitching green and bunkers are all available and great.

Lín jīnglǐ:　Nín mùqián chéngjì rúhé?

○ 林经理：　您目前成绩如何？

Manager Lin:　What's your best achievement till now?

Kǎ'ěr:　Wǒ mùqián chàdiǎn shì shíliù, zuì hǎo chéngjì bāshíyī gān.

● 卡尔：　我目前差点是 16，最好成绩 81 杆。

Karl:　Now my handicap is 16, and the best achievement is 81 clubs.

Lín jīnglǐ:　Gāoshǒu a!

○ 林经理：　高手啊！

Manager Lin:　A master-hand!

Kǎ'ěr:　Nǎli nǎli.

● 卡尔：　哪里哪里。

Karl:　 Thank you.

Tāmen láidào fāqiúqū.

他们来到发球区。

They come to the service area.

Qiútóng:　Xiānsheng, nín èr wèi shéi xiān kāi qiú?

○ 球童：　先生，您二位谁先开球？

Caddy:　Sir, who will be the first one to tee off?

Kǎ'ěr:　Lín jīnglǐ, nín xiān qǐng!

● 卡尔：　林经理，您先请！

Karl:　Manager Lin, you first!

Lín jīnglǐ:　Nà wǒ jiù bú kèqi le.

○ 林经理：　那我就不客气了。

Manager Lin:　OK.

Dǎ qiú guòchéng zhōng.

打球过程中。

During playing...

Kǎ'ěr:　Hǎo! Yì gān shàng guǒlǐng, lìhai! Wǒ de yālì hěn dà ya!

● 卡尔：　好！一杆上果岭，厉害！我的压力很大呀！

Karl:　Great! Go to the putting green with only one club. You are giving me too much pressure.

Lín jīnglǐ:
○ 林经理：今天手感不错。我的优势在果岭，一上果岭

Jīntiān shǒugǎn búcuò. Wǒ de yōushì zài guǒlǐng, yí shàng guǒlǐng

jiù gèng yǒu xìnxīn le.
就更有信心了。

Manager Lin: Good handle today. My advantage is in putting green and I feel more confident once we are on the putting green.

Kǎ'ěr:
● 卡尔：看我的！

Kàn wǒ de!

Karl: Look at me!

Tāmen biān zǒu biān liáo.
他们边走边聊。
They are walking and chatting.

Kǎ'ěr:
○ 卡尔：林经理，您是什么时候开始打高尔夫球的？

Lín jīnglǐ, nín shì shénme shíhou kāishǐ dǎ gāo'ěrfūqiú de?

Karl: Manager Lin, when did you begin to play golf?

Lín jīnglǐ:
● 林经理：6年前，朋友推荐的，越打越喜欢。

Liù nián qián, péngyou tuījiàn de, yuè dǎ yuè xǐhuan.

Manager Lin: Six years ago, a friend recommended it to me. The more I play it, the better I like it.

Kǎ'ěr:
○ 卡尔：是啊，阳光、空气、绿色，天然的大氧吧，人的

Shì a, yángguāng、kōngqì、lǜsè, tiānrán de dà yǎngbā, rén de

xīnqíng hǎo, shēntǐ yě gèng jiànkāng le!
心情好，身体也更健康了！

Karl: Yes. Sunshine, air, green, and a huge natural oxygen bar. Good mood can keep you healthy.

Lín jīnglǐ:
● 林经理：而且通过打球，我还认识了很多朋友。

Érqiě tōngguò dǎ qiú, wǒ hái rènshile hěn duō péngyou.

Manager Lin: I have also made many friends by playing golf.

Kǎ'ěr:	Xià zhōuliù yǒu kòngr ma? Wǒ yuēle liǎng ge qiúyǒu hē chá, nín yě
○ 卡尔:	下周六有空儿吗？我约了两个球友喝茶，您也
	lái, rènshi rènshi, rúhé?
	来，认识认识，如何？
Karl:	Are you free next Saturday? I've invited two golf friends to have tea. Would you like to come and meet them?

Lín jīnglǐ:	Xià zhōuliù wǒmen gōngsī de rénlì zīyuánbù gěi yuángōngmen ānpáile
● 林经理:	下周六我们公司的人力资源部给员工们安排了
	yí cì tuòzhǎn xùnliàn. Wǒ děi qù kànkan. Yǒu jīhuì zài yuē ba!
	一次拓展训练。我得去看看。有机会再约吧！
Manager Lin:	The Human Resources Department of our company has arranged a field training for the staff next Saturday. I need to have a look. Maybe next time.

Kǎ'ěr:	Kàn nín fāngbiàn!
○ 卡尔:	看您方便！
Karl:	At your convenience.

生词 Shēngcí	**New Words**		
1. 俱乐部	jùlèbù	N	club
2. 预约	yùyuē	V	to reserve
3. 会员	huìyuán	N	member
4. 卡	kǎ	N	card
5. 安排	ānpái	V	to arrange
6. 球童	qiútóng	N	caddy
7. 为	wèi	Prep	for
8. 服务	fúwù	V	to serve
9. 球包	qiúbāo	N	golf bag
10. 场地	chǎngdì	N	site
11. 洞	dòng	N	hole

12. 杆	gān	N	pole
13. 国际	guójì	Adj	international
14. 标准	biāozhǔn	Adj	standard
15. 球场	qiúchǎng	N	course
16. 属于	shǔyú	V	to belong to
17. 山地	shāndì	N	hilly area
18. 型	xíng	N	model
19. 练习	liànxí	V/N	to practice; exercise
20. 推	tuī	V	to push
21. 果岭	guǒlǐng	N	green
22. 切	qiē	V	to cut
23. 沙坑	shākēng	N	bunker
24. 目前	mùqián	N	at present
25. 成绩	chéngjì	N	score
26. 如何	rúhé	Pr	how
27. 差点	chàdiǎn	N	handicap
28. 高手	gāoshǒu	N	expert
29. 哪里	nǎli	Pr	not really
30. 开	kāi	V	to begin, to start
31. 球	qiú	N	ball
32. 厉害	lìhai	Adj	awesome
33. 压力	yālì	N	pressure
34. 手感	shǒugǎn	N	the feel of touching
35. 优势	yōushì	N	advantage
36. 信心	xìnxīn	N	confidence
37. 高尔夫球	gāo'ěrfūqiú	N	golf
38. 推荐	tuījiàn	V	to recommend
39. 越……越……	yuè……yuè……		more…more…

40. 阳光	yángguāng	N	sunshine
41. 天然	tiānrán	Adj	natural
42. 氧吧	yǎngbā	N	oxygen bar
43. 心情	xīnqíng	N	mood
44. 健康	jiànkāng	Adj	healthy
45. 而且	érqiě	Conj	moreover
46. 通过	tōngguò	Prep	through
47. 周六	zhōuliù	N	Saturday
48. 约	yuē	V	to date
49. 球友	qiúyǒu	N	golfer
50. 人力	rénlì	N	manpower
51. 资源	zīyuán	N	resource
52. 部	bù	N	department
53. 拓展	tuòzhǎn	V	to expand
54. 训练	xùnliàn	V	to train
55. 机会	jīhuì	N	chance

注释 Zhùshì **Notes**

1 您几位一起打球？ How many of you are going to play golf?

"您几位"，询问人数，一些消费场所的服务人员常用，是较为正式的说法，比"你们几个人"更有礼貌。有时也可以用"您几位 + V+ O"，针对具体的事情询问人员的数量。

"您几位" is used to ask the number of people. It is often used by waiters at areas of consumption and is more formal and polite than "你们几个人". Sometimes "您几位 + V + O" is also used to ask the number of people in a specific situation.

注意："几"也可以表示不定的数目，不表示询问，如"您几位"也可以用在陈述句中。"您二位"是当对方有两个人时的称呼，而"您几位"是当对方的人数超过两人时不具体称呼人数的说法，如："您几位现在点菜吗"、"这是您几位的饮料"。

Note: "儿" is also used to indicate an indefinite number, not an interrogation. "您几位" can also be used in a declarative sentence. "您二位" is used to address two listeners, while "您几位" is used when there are more than two listeners, for example, "您几位现在点菜吗", "这是您几位的饮料"。

2   现在安排球童为您服务。   I will send a caddy to help you.

"为"，介词，表示行为的对象，可以带名词、代词，组成介词结构作状语，修饰动词。例如：

"为", a preposition, indicates the object of the action. It can be followed by a noun or pronoun to form a prepositional structure, serving as the adverbial to modify the verb. For example,

①卡尔为明明买了生日礼物。

②我很希望（xīwàng, to hope）能为你们公司做点儿事儿。

③我们很高兴能为您服务。

3   先生，请您看一下，这是您的球包吗？   Sir, please have a look, is this your golf bag?

"下（儿）"，动量词。动量词是表示动作或变化次数的量词，大多用在动词后作补语。常用的动量词有"下、次、遍、回、趟（tàng）"等。例如：

"下（儿）" is a measure word for actions. Measure words for actions indicate the number of times an action or a change happened and are mostly used after verbs as complements. The most frequently used ones include "下", "次", "遍", "回", "趟", etc. For example,

①我听了三遍课文的 MP3。

②他去过三次上海。

③小张打（dǎ, to hit）了小王一下。

④长城我去过三回。

4   您目前成绩如何？   What's your best achievement till now?

"如何"，疑问代词，"怎么、怎么样"的意思。用在书面语或比较正式的交际场合。例如：

"如何", an interrogative pronoun, means "how". It is usually used in written Chinese or formal occasions. For example,

①您最近身体如何？

②他打球打得如何？

③北京冬天的天气如何？

5 哪里哪里。 Thank you.

"哪里"，代词。这里不表示疑问，而表示否认，谦辞。当对方夸奖自己的时候用，表示谦虚，是交际场合的客套话。例如：

The pronoun "哪里" doesn't indicate an interrogation, but a negation. It is a self-depreciatory expression. This polite remark is used when the speaker is praised by another person. For example,

A：您汉语说得真好！

B：哪里哪里，我还差（chà, to differ）得远呢！

因为这种用法是用来对别人的夸奖的一种否定，所以，通常"哪里哪里"用在同辈人之间，晚辈对长辈用会显得不够客气。此外，现在很多中国人特别是年轻人也常用"谢谢"来回答夸奖。

This usage is a negation of other people's praise. As a result, "哪里哪里" is usually used among peers and is not polite to the seniors. In addition, many Chinese, especially young people often use "谢谢" in response to the compliment from others.

6 看我的！ Look at me!

"看我的"，常单说。表示向别人显示自己的决心和本领，含有夸耀和逞能的意味。

"看我的" is often used by itself to show one's determination and capability, with an implication of showing off .

7 林经理，您是什么时候开始打高尔夫球的？

Manager Lin, when did you begin to play golf?

"是……的"句，强调说明做某件事情的人、时间、地点、方式等，被强调的是已经发生的事情。"是……的"中间一般是动词、状动短语、主谓短语等。"是"常用在谓语前，有时也用在主语前，有时还可以省略。否定式是在"是"前加"不"，这时"是"不能省略。例如：

"是……的" sentence is used to emphasize who, when, where or how something happened. In "是……的", a verb, an adverbial verbal phrase or a subject-predicate phrase is generally used between "是" and "的". "是" is often used before the predicate, or before the subject or omitted sometimes. Its negative forms is placing "不" before "是". In this case, "是" is not omitted. For example,

① 我（是）今年 2 月到北京的。（强调时间 To emphasize the time. ）

② 这个杯子是在家乐福买的。（强调地点 To emphasize the place. ）

③ 是卡尔告诉我的。（强调人 To emphasize the people. ）

④ 张远是坐火车去上海的。（强调方式 To emphasize the manner. ）

⑤ 这些字不是康爱丽写的，是卡尔写的。（本句不是否定动作"写"，而是否定前后对比的焦点部分　This sentence doesn't negate the action "写", but the part that is in contrast.）

"是……的"句的陈述形式和疑问形式如下：

The declarative and interrogative forms of the sentence pattern "是……的" is as follows:

陈述句 Declarative sentence	疑问句 Interrogative sentence
我（是）今年2月到北京的。	你是什么时候到北京的？
这个杯子是在家乐福买的。	这个杯子是在哪儿买的？
张远是坐火车去上海的。	张远是怎么去上海的？
这些字是卡尔写的。	这些字是谁写的？
这些字不是康爱丽写的，是卡尔写的。	这些字是康爱丽写的吗？

注意："是……的"不能和表示完成的动态助词"了"并用。例如：

Note: "是……的" cannot be used together with the aspect particle "了". For example,

⑥ 我是去年来了北京的。（×）

⑦ 我是去年来北京的。（√）

8 越打越喜欢。**The more I play it, the better I like it.**

"越 A 越 B"，表示 B 的程度随着 A 的情况的发展而加深，意思更进了一层。"越"，副词，表示程度随着条件的发展而发展，一般不单用。前后两部分 A、B 的主语可以相同，也可以不同。例如：

"越 A 越 B" indicates the degree of B grows with the development of A. "越", an adverb, indicates the degree grows with the development of the condition. Generally, "越" is not used on its own. The subjects of A and B can be the same or different. For example,

① 我越看越喜欢。

② 他越想越觉得高兴。

③ 你别说了！你越说，他越生气。

注意：第二个"越"后的动词、形容词前不能用程度副词修饰。

Note: The verb or adjective after the second "越" cannot be modified by an adverb of degree.

9 而且通过打球，我还认识了很多朋友。

　　I have also made many friends by playing golf.

　　"而且"，连词，表示意思更进一层。如本句是顺着前面所说的内容介绍打高尔夫球更多的好处。

　　"而且", a conjunction, indicates furthermore in meaning.This sentence follows what is mentioned before to present more benefits of playing golf.

　　"而且" 可以连接并列的动词、形容词、小句等。常常有连词 "不但、不仅" 在前一分句，构成 "不但 / 不仅……，而且……" 的句式，表示一种递进的关系。"而且" 连接小句时，后面常有 "还、也、更" 等副词。例如：

　　"而且" is used to connect the coordinate verbs, adjectives, or clauses, etc. The conjunction "不但" or "不仅" is often used in the preceding clause, forming the sentence pattern "不但 / 不仅……，而且……" to indicate a progressive relationship. When "而且" connects two clauses, it is often followed by an adverb like "还", "也" or "更". For example,

　　① 他会说汉语，而且说得也很流利。

　　② 他不但很聪明，而且还很努力。

　　③ 你不仅要去，而且还要去得比大家早。

10 而且通过打球，我还认识了很多朋友。

　　I have also made many friends by playing golf.

　　"通过"，介词，引进人或事物作为动作的媒介和手段。"通过"后可以带名词、动词（短语）、小句等。"通过"可以用在主语前。例如：

　　The preposition "通过" introduces a person or thing, which is the medium or means of doing something. "通过" can be followed by a noun, a verb (phrase), or a clause, etc. and can be used before the subject. For example,

　　① 通过学习，他的汉语水平提高（tígāo, to improve）了。

　　② 通过上网，我了解（liǎojiě, to find out）到了更多的信息。

　　③ 通过康爱丽介绍，卡尔认识了李明明。

11 有机会再约吧！　　Maybe next time.

　　"再"，副词，表示又一次，指一个动作（或状态）的重复或继续。多指还没有实现的或经常性的动作。作状语，修饰动词。我们在第五单元课文三中也学过这个用法。例如：

　　The adverb "再" indicates "again", that is, the repetition or continuation of an action (or a state). It often refers to something that is undone or something that happens on a regular basis. It is used as an adverbial to modify a verb. We have learned it in Text 3, Unit 5. For example,

① 时间还早，你再坐一会儿吧。

② 欢迎你下次再来。

③ 咱们还能再去一次故宫吗？

④ 我还想再见到你。

⑤ 这个问题我再想想。

12 高尔夫球运动常用术语　Frequently used golf terms

标准杆	biāozhǔngān	par
总杆数	zǒnggānshù	gross
差点	chàdiǎn	handicap
记分卡	jìfēnkǎ	score card
球道	qiúdào	fairway
进场	jìnchǎng	course
发球台	fāqiútái	tee ground
球洞	qiúdòng	hole
长洞	chángdòng	long hole
短洞	duǎndòng	short hole
粗草区	cūcǎoqū	rough
沙坑	shākēng	bunker
池塘	chítáng	water harzard
码	mǎ	yard
一杆进洞	yì gān jìn dòng	hole in one
球袋	qiúdài	bag

Huáiróu Tuòzhǎn Xùnliàn Xíngchéng Ānpái

怀柔拓展训练行程安排

Schedule of the field training in huairou

3

Kèwén Sān

课文三

Text 3

- **周五　Friday**

  16：30　在公司门口集合

  Assemble at the gate of the company

  16：30～19：00　到达怀柔拓展基地，入住宾馆

  Arrive at the field training base in Huairou, and check in the hotel

  19：15～20：15　晚餐　Dinner

  20：30～22：30　分组热身，选队长、确定口号和队歌

  Divide into groups, warm up, select the group leaders, decide the slogans and songs

  for the groups

  23：00　休息　Recess

- **周六　Saturday**

  7：00～7：30　晨练　Morning exercises

  7：45～8：15　早餐　Breakfast

  8：15～10：15　拓展项目1——水上课程：游泳

  Field training program 1 — water course: swimming

10：30～12：30　拓展项目2——水上课程：跳水

Field training program 2 — water course: diving

12：30～13：30　午餐、午休　Lunch and the noon break

13：30～14：00　集合　Assemble

14：00～16：00　拓展项目3——野外课程：爬山

Field training program 3 — field course: mountain climbing

16：15～18：15　一天拓展项目讲评

Comment on the the training of the day

18：30～19：00　动手建营、搭帐篷　Building the tents

19：00～20：00　晚餐　Supper

20：00～23：00　篝火晚会、卡拉OK晚会

Campfire party and karaoke party

23：00　休息　Recess

● 周日　Sunday

7：00～7：45　晨练　Morning exercises

8：00～8：30　早餐　Breakfast

8：30～9：00　收营　Dismount the tents

9：00～13：00　拓展项目4——场地课程：攀岩

Field training program 4 — ground course: rock-climbing

13：00～14：30　午餐、午休　Lunch and the noon break

14：30～17：00　总结　Summary

17：00　返回，活动结束　Return and the training drawing to a close

○ 注意事项　Note：

1. 着装要求：请穿运动服、运动鞋。

Wear sportwear and gym shoes.

2. 服从教练安排，不得擅自行动。

Do what is told by your coach and do not act without prior consent.

3. 爱护环境，不乱丢垃圾。

Protect the environment and do not litter.

生词 Shēngcí New Words

1. 行程	xíngchéng	N	travel route, itinerary
2. 周五	zhōuwǔ	N	Friday
3. 门口	ménkǒu	N	doorway, entrance, gate
4. 集合	jíhé	V	to gather
5. 到达	dàodá	V	to arrive (at / in)
6. 基地	jīdì	N	base
7. 入住	rùzhù	V	to check in
8. 宾馆	bīnguǎn	N	hotel
9. 晚餐	wǎncān	N	supper, dinner
10. 分	fēn	V	to divide
11. 组	zǔ	N	group
12. 热身	rèshēn	V	to warm up
13. 选	xuǎn	V	to choose, to select
14. 队长	duìzhǎng	N	team leader
15. 确定	quèdìng	V	to decide
16. 口号	kǒuhào	N	slogan
17. 队歌	duìgē	N	song of the group or team
18. 晨练	chénliàn	V	to do morning exercises
19. 早餐	zǎocān	N	breakfast
20. 项目	xiàngmù	N	program
21. 水上	shuǐshàng	N	aquatic
22. 课程	kèchéng	N	course
23. 跳水	tiàoshuǐ	V	to dive
24. 午餐	wǔcān	N	lunch
25. 午休	wǔxiū	V	to take a noon break
26. 野外	yěwài	Adj	field, outdoor

27. 爬山	pá shān	V O	to climb a mountain
28. 讲评	jiǎngpíng	V	to comment
29. 动手	dòng shǒu	V//O	to get doing
30. 建	jiàn	V	to build
31. 营	yíng	N	camp
32. 搭	dā	V	to set up
33. 帐篷	zhàngpeng	N	tent
34. 篝火	gōuhuǒ	N	campfire
35. 晚会	wǎnhuì	N	party
36. 卡拉OK	kǎlā-OK		karaoke
37. 周日	zhōurì	N	Sunday
38. 收	shōu	V	to bring to an end, to stop
39. 攀岩	pānyán	V	to climb the rock
40. 总结	zǒngjié	V	to summarize
41. 返回	fǎnhuí	V	to return
42. 结束	jiéshù	V	to end
43. 注意	zhùyì	V	to pay attention to
44. 事项	shìxiàng	N	item
45. 着装	zhuózhuāng	V/N	to wear (clothes, etc.); clothing
46. 要求	yāoqiú	V/N	to request; request
47. 运动服	yùndòngfú	N	sports suit / wear
48. 运动鞋	yùndòngxié	N	gym shoes
49. 服从	fúcóng	V	to obey
50. 教练	jiàoliàn	N	coach
51. 不得	bù dé		should not
52. 擅自	shànzì	Adv	without prior consent
53. 行动	xíngdòng	V/N	to act; action
54. 爱护	àihù	V	to cherish and protect

55. 环境	huánjìng	N	environment
56. 乱	luàn	Adj	messy
57. 丢	diū	V	to throw
58. 垃圾	lājī	N	garbage

专有名词 Zhuānyǒu míngcí **A Proper Noun**

| 怀柔 | Huáiróu | suburban district in the northeast of Beijing |

注释 Zhùshì **Notes**

服从教练安排，不得擅自行动。

Do what is told by your coach and don't act without prior consent.

"得（dé）"，能愿动词，表示"许可"的意思，多用在书面语中。在陈述句中一般只用否定形式。"不得"表示行动不被许可。例如：

"得" is an optative verb to indicate the permission and is often used in written Chinese. In a declarative sentence, it's generally used in its negative form. "不得" means the action is not allowed. For example,

① 不得随地（suídì, everywhere）吐痰（tǔ tán, to spit）！

② 不得乱扔果皮（guǒpí, peel）纸屑（zhǐxiè, scrap of paper）！

③ 每条船（chuán, boat）不得超过四人。

注意：当表达肯定的意思时用"可以"。

Note：Its affirmative form is "可以".

练习 Liànxí **Exercises**

一 跟读生词，注意发音和声调。
Read the new words after the teacher and pay attention to your pronunciation and tones.

二 跟读课文，注意语音语调。
Read the texts after the teacher and pay attention to your pronunciation and intonation.

三 学生分组，分角色朗读课文一、二；分段朗读课文三。
Divide the students into groups and read Texts 1 & 2 in roles, Text 3 paragraph by paragraph in turns.

四 学生分组，不看书，分角色表演课文一、二。
Divide the students into groups and play the roles in Texts 1 & 2 without referring to the book.

五 角色扮演。（提示：角色可以互换。）
Role playing. (Note: the roles can be exchanged.)

1. 关于运动：两个学生一组，互相询问喜欢什么运动并说明原因。用课文里学过的词语和句子完成一段对话。

   About sports: Students work in pairs to ask each other about their favorite sports and the reasons they like these sports. Complete a dialogue with the words and sentences you learned from the texts.

2. 关于爱好：两个学生一组，互相询问有什么爱好，并且向对方介绍自己有这种爱好的原因和情况。用课文里学过的词语和句子完成一段对话。

   About hobbies: Students work in pairs and ask each others' hobbies. Tell each other the reasons and how they have such hobbies. Use the words, phrases and sentences in the texts to complete a dialogue.

3. 两人一组完成一段对话：去健身房或者去打高尔夫。

   Students work in pairs to complete a dialogue: going to the gym or playing golf.

六 复述课文一和课文二。
Retell Texts 1 & 2.

七 替换练习。
Substitution drills.

① 我 一 听 就 懂。

夏天我	放假	回家
我每天	起床	去上课
我哥哥	洗澡	唱歌
我	写作业	想睡觉

② 除了 中国菜 以外，我 还 喜欢日本菜。

看书	他	常常看电影
游泳	她	打网球（wǎngqiú, tennis）
中国	我同学	去过美国
啤酒	他朋友	喜欢喝可乐

③ 我 游泳 游 得 很好。

我朋友	打球	打	很棒
我妈妈	做饭（zuò fàn, to cook）	做	很好吃
我弟弟	考试	考	很差（chà, inferior）
他	跑步	跑	很快

④ 现在安排球童 为 您 服务。

我明天安排老师	你们	上课
她	她的先生（xiānsheng, husband）	买了一件生日礼物
公司	员工	安排了拓展训练
你能	我们	唱一首歌吗

⑤ 通过 <u>打球</u>，<u>我</u> 认识了很多朋友。

学中文	我朋友	爱上了中国
锻炼	他	比以前瘦了
上网	她	找到了房子
旅行	我	了解了不同的文化（wénhuà, culture）

⑥ 不得 <u>擅自行动</u>。

吸烟

停车（tíng chē, to park）

大声喧哗（xuānhuá, to make an uproar）

乱扔果皮纸屑

八 用下面的词语组成句子。
Make sentences with the following words and expressions.

① 什么　打算　周末　做　你

② 看电影　还　我　听音乐　和　喜欢

③ 爱好　看书　是　我　旅行　的

④ 几　打球　一起　您　位

⑤ 您　什么　开始　是　时候　打球　的

⑥ 一次　公司　拓展训练　了　员工们　给　安排

⑦ 更　身体　的　健康　了　人

九 用带"得"的程度补语完成对话。

Complete the dialogues with the complement of degree "得".

1 A：你喜欢喝汤吗？这家饭馆的汤做＿＿＿＿＿＿＿＿＿＿＿＿。

B：＿＿＿＿＿＿＿＿＿＿＿＿＿＿＿＿＿＿。

A：那我们点个汤吧。

2 A：昨天晚上的电影演＿＿＿＿＿＿＿＿＿＿＿＿＿＿＿？

B：＿＿＿＿＿＿＿＿＿＿＿＿＿＿＿＿＿。你为什么没去看？

A：我女朋友要我和她去买东西，没时间看电影。

3 A：昨天晚上你几点睡觉的？

B：十二点。

A：＿＿＿＿＿＿＿＿＿＿＿＿＿＿＿＿＿？

B：＿＿＿＿＿＿＿＿＿＿＿＿＿＿＿＿＿。

十 用"是……的"回答问题。

Answer the questions with "是……的".

Example: A：你是什么时候来北京的？

B：我是上个星期来北京的。（上个星期）

1 A：你的汉语是在哪儿学的？

B：＿＿＿＿＿＿＿＿＿＿＿＿＿＿＿＿＿。（学校）

2 A：你是怎么去飞机场的？

B：＿＿＿＿＿＿＿＿＿＿＿＿＿＿＿＿＿。（开车）

3 A：你昨天是跟谁一起去吃饭的？

B：＿＿＿＿＿＿＿＿＿＿＿＿＿＿＿＿＿。（朋友）

4 A：这件毛衣（máoyī, sweater）是谁给你买的？

B：＿＿＿＿＿＿＿＿＿＿＿＿＿＿＿＿＿。（我妈妈）

5 A：你的朋友是从哪儿来的？

B：＿＿＿＿＿＿＿＿＿＿＿＿＿＿＿＿＿。（美国）

十一 用"越……越……"改写句子。

Rewrite the sentences with "越……越……".

Example: 我的钱　多　好 ——→ 我的钱越多越好。

① 咱们的朋友　多　好 ——→

② 公寓离学校　近　好 ——→

③ 四川菜　辣　好吃 ——→

④ 我的朋友　吃　胖 ——→

⑤ 我同学　学汉语　喜欢 ——→

十二 阅读理解。

Reading comprehension.

　　大王和小王都喜欢运动，大王是小王的哥哥。

　　大王周末常常去踢足球，有时候还跟朋友一起打篮球。朋友都很忙的话，大王就自己一个人去跑步。因为常常运动，大王的身体棒极了。他今年快四十岁了，可是看起来就像二十多岁一样。

　　小王也喜欢运动，可是他跟他哥哥大王不一样，他只喜欢看别人运动，不喜欢自己运动。电视上一有足球赛或者篮球赛，小王就坐在沙发上看电视，一看就是几个钟头，有时候连饭都不吃。他今年才三十岁，可是越来越胖，看起来像四十岁一样。

生词　Shēngcí　**New Words**

1. 快	kuài	Adv	nearly
2. 看起来	kàn qilai		to look, to seem to be
3. 像……一样	xiàng……yíyàng		to look like

4. 或者	huòzhě	Conj	or
5. 才	cái	Adv	only, merely, just

判断正误：

Decide whether the following statements are true (√) or false (×):

(　　) ❶ 大王看起来像小王的弟弟。

(　　) ❷ 除了踢足球以外，大王还喜欢别的运动。

(　　) ❸ 大王常常跟小王一起打篮球。

(　　) ❹ 因为小王常常打球，所以他的身体不错。

(　　) ❺ 要是电视上有球赛，小王不会去看电影或者听音乐。

十三 谈谈你在中国的生活。

Talk about your life in China.

提示：你什么时候起床？什么时候去上课？什么时候上班？早还是晚？你汉语学得怎

么样？你周末常常做什么？生活得愉快不愉快？

要求：用带"得"的程度补语。

Prompt: What time do you get up? What time do you go to class? What time do you go

to work? Early or late? How do you learn Chinese? What do you usually do at

weekends? Are you happy?

Requirement: Please use the complement of degree "得" in your passage.

十四 扩展练习。

Expansion exercise.

1. 谈论运动：下面的方框中是一些谈论运动时常用的句子。两人一组，在下面给出的

"任务项目"中选择一两种，模仿这些句式完成对话。

Talking about sports: In the following box, there are some frequently used sentences to talk

about sports. Students work in pairs and choose one or two tasks from the following items.

Follow the sentence patterns to complete the dialogue.

A	B
你每天锻炼身体吗？	对。我很喜欢运动。
你最喜欢什么运动？	我最喜欢打篮球和游泳。
你篮球打得怎么样？	打得还可以，游泳也游得不错。
你会踢足球吗？	不会，可是我喜欢看足球比赛。
你是球迷（mí, fan）吧？	对，我每个星期天都去体育场（tǐyùchǎng, stadium）。如果买不到票，就看电视。

任务项目：

打排球（páiqiú, volleyball） 打网球

打棒球（bàngqiú, baseball） 打台球（táiqiú, billiards）

打羽毛球（yǔmáoqiú, badminton） 打乒乓球（pīngpāngqiú, table tennis）

打保龄球（bǎolíngqiú, bowling） 打太极拳（tàijíquán, Taichi）

滑冰 滑雪

2. 谈论爱好：下面的方框中是一些谈论爱好时常用的句子。两人一组，在下面给出的
   "任务项目"中选择一两种，模仿这些句式完成对话。

Talking about hobbies: In the following box, there are some frequently used sentences to talk about hobbies. Students work in pairs and choose one or two tasks from the following items. Follow the sentence patterns to complete the dialogue.

A	B
你有什么爱好？	我喜欢画画儿。
除了画画儿以外，你还喜欢做什么？	我还爱照相（zhào xiàng, to take pictures）。
你的爱好是什么？	我的爱好是听音乐、看电影。
你会弹（tán, to play）钢琴（gāngqín, piano）吗？	我会弹钢琴。
你钢琴弹得怎么样？	我弹得还不错。
你学钢琴学多长时间了？	我学钢琴差不多三年了。

任务项目：

唱歌 跳舞（tiào wǔ, to dance）

下棋（xià qí, to play chess） 旅行

看书 看电视

逛街 买东西

十五 完成任务：请用课文中学过的词语和句子完成任务。
Complete the tasks: Please complete the tasks with the words and sentences you have learned in the texts.

课后完成 (Homework)：

通过网络了解中国公司为员工安排什么样的活动。

Get to know from the Internet what activities Chinese companies may arrange for their staff.

课堂讨论 (Class Discussion)：

1. 这些公司为什么要安排这些活动？你对这些活动有什么看法？
Class discussion: Why do these companies hold such activities? What's your opinion?

2. 你们国家的公司或者你所在的公司会为员工安排什么样的活动？为什么？你的看法是什么？
What activities the companies of your mother country or the company you work for arrange for the employees? Why? What's your opinion?

3. 对比中外公司为员工安排的活动有什么异同。
Compare the differences and similarities between the activit Chinese companies and foreign companies arrange for their employees.

生词总表
Vocabulary

（最后一列表示生词所在单元和课号，如"103"表示第十单元课文三）

（The last column indicates the unit number and text number of the new word, for example, "103" indicates the new word is in Text 3, Unit 10.）

A

1	爱好	àihào	N	hobby	101
2	爱护	àihù	V	to cherish and protect	103
3	安排	ānpái	V	to arrange	102

B

4	把	bǎ	Prep	*used to introduce "S + V + Comp" structure*	091
5	白天	báitiān	N	daytime	093
6	百合	bǎihé	N	lily	083
7	办	bàn	V	to hold (a party, etc.)	083
8	帮忙	bāng máng	V//O	to help, to do (sb.) a favour	062
9	杯	bēi	N	cup, glass	072
10	北边	běibian	N	north	061
11	北方	běifāng	N	the north	093
12	比	bǐ	Prep	*used for comparison*	092
13	比较	bǐjiào	Adv	comparatively	092
14	比赛	bǐsài	N	game, match	101
15	边	bian	Suf	*suffix of location words*	061
16	标准	biāozhǔn	Adj	standard	102
17	别人	biéren	Pr	other people	101
18	宾馆	bīnguǎn	N	hotel	103

19	不错	búcuò	Adj	not bad	071
20	不过	búguò	Conj	but	082
21	不用	búyòng	Adv	not need	062
22	不得	bù dé		should not	103
23	不好意思	bù hǎoyìsi	IE	to be sorry	072
24	部	bù	N	department	102

C

25	菜	cài	N	dish	072
26	菜单	càidān	N	menu	072
27	参加	cānjiā	V	to take part in, to attend	083
28	餐厅	cāntīng	N	restaurant	071
29	差不多	chàbuduō	Adv	almost	063
30	差点	chàdiǎn	N	handicap	102
31	长	cháng	Adj	long	063
32	常客	chángkè	N	regular customer	071
33	场	chǎng	M	*a measure word for activities*	091
34	场地	chǎngdì	N	site	102
35	超市	chāoshì	N	supermarket	061
36	晨练	chénliàn	V	to do morning exercises	103
37	成绩	chéngjì	N	score	102
38	成千上万	chéng qiān shàng wàn		thousands of	093
39	吃饭	chī fàn	V O	to have a meal	071
40	吃素	chīsù	V	to be a vegetarian	072
41	除了	chúle	Prep	except (for)	101
42	川菜	chuāncài	N	Sichuan cuisine	071
43	春天	chūntiān	N	spring	092

44	次	cì	M	time	072
45	促销	cùxiāo	V	to promote the sales of goods	091

D

46	搭	dā	V	to set up	103
47	达到	dádào	V	to reach	093
48	打	dǎ	V	to make (a phone call)	082
49	打	dǎ	V	to play	101
50	打算	dǎsuàn	V/N	to plan; plan	101
51	打折	dǎ zhé	V//O	to give a discount	071
52	大概	dàgài	Adv	probably	063
53	蛋炒饭	dànchǎofàn	N	fried rice with eggs	072
54	蛋糕	dàngāo	N	cake	083
55	到	dào	V	to arrive	061
56	到达	dàodá	V	to arrive (at / in)	103
57	的话	dehuà	Pt	*a particle indicating supposition*	063
58	得	děi	OpV	have to, need	063
59	低	dī	Adj	low	091
60	地址	dìzhǐ	N	address	082
61	第	dì	Suf	*used before integers to indicate order, such as lst, 10th*	061
62	点	diǎn	V	to order (dishes)	072
63	电话	diànhuà	N	telephone	071
64	电视	diànshì	N	television	101
65	电梯	diàntī	N	elevator	062
66	电影	diànyǐng	N	movie	101
67	订	dìng	V	to order, to book	083
68	定	dìng	V	to settle, to decide	082
69	丢	diū	V	to throw	103

70	东西	dōngxi	N	thing	063
71	冬天	dōngtiān	N	winter	092
72	懂	dǒng	V	to understand	072
73	动手	dòng shǒu	V//O	to get doing	103
74	洞	dòng	N	hole	102
75	堵车	dǔ chē	V//O	to have a traffic jam	063
76	度	dù	N	degree	093
77	短	duǎn	Adj	short	093
78	短信	duǎnxìn	N	message	082
79	锻炼	duànliàn	V	to have exercises	101
80	队歌	duìgē	N	song of the group or team	103
81	队长	duìzhǎng	N	team leader	103
82	多	duō	Adv	how	063

E

83	而且	érqiě	Conj	moreover	102

F

84	发票	fāpiào	N	receipt	063
85	返回	fǎnhuí	V	to return	103
86	饭馆（儿)	fànguǎn (r)	N	restaurant	071
87	放心	fàng xīn	V//O	to set one's mind at rest	091
88	飞机	fēijī	N	plane, airplane	063
89	分	fēn	V	to divide	103
90	分钟	fēnzhōng	N	minute	063
91	份	fèn	M	*a measure word*	072
92	风	fēng	N	wind	091
93	风景	fēngjǐng	N	landscape, scenery	092
94	风沙	fēngshā	N	sand blown by the wind, sandstorm	093

95	服从	fúcóng	V	to obey	103
96	服务	fúwù	V	to serve	102
97	服务员	fúwùyuán	N	waiter / waitress	072
98	附近	fùjìn	N	near, nearby	061

G

99	改天	gǎitiān	Adv	someday	092
100	干燥	gānzào	Adj	dry	093
101	杆	gān	N	pole	102
102	高	gāo	Adj	high	091
103	高尔夫球	gāo'ěrfūqiú	N	golf	102
104	高手	gāoshǒu	N	expert	102
105	高速	gāosù	Adj	high speed	063
106	各	gè	Pr	each, every	093
107	各个	gègè	Pr	each, every	093
108	跟	gēn	Prep	with, and	092
109	更	gèng	Adv	more, even more	061
110	篝火	gōuhuǒ	N	campfire	103
111	拐	guǎi	V	to turn	061
112	关心	guānxīn	V	to care, to concern	091
113	国产	guóchǎn	Adj	made in one's own country	062
114	国际	guójì	Adj	international	102
115	国家	guójiā	N	country	093
116	果岭	guǒlǐng	N	green	102
117	果汁	guǒzhī	N	juice	072
118	过	guò	V	to cross	061
119	过	guo	AP	*used after a verb to indicate the completion of an action*	083

H

120	还是	háishi	Adv	(*expressing hope*) had better	072
121	旱鸭子	hànyāzi	N	landlubber	101
122	航站楼	hángzhànlóu	N	terminal	063
123	号码	hàomǎ	N	number	071
124	喝	hē	V	to drink	072
125	合作	hézuò	N	to cooperate	082
126	和	hé	Conj	and	061
127	和	hé	Prep	and, with	082
128	红酒	hóngjiǔ	N	red wine	062
129	红叶	hóngyè	N	red leaf	092
130	后天	hòutiān	N	the day after tomorrow	082
131	户外	hùwài	N	outdoor	091
132	花儿	huār	N	flower	083
133	滑冰	huá bīng	V//O	to skate	092
134	滑雪	huá xuě	V//O	to ski	092
135	环境	huánjìng	N	environment	103
136	黄金周	huángjīnzhōu	N	golden week	093
137	回	huí	V	to return, to reply	081
138	回来	huílai	V	to be back, to return	081
139	会	huì	OpV	can, will	083
140	会员	huìyuán	N	member	102
141	活动	huódòng	N	activity	091
142	火	huǒ	Adj	brisk, prosperous	071
143	货架	huòjià	N	shelf	062

J

| 144 | 机场 | jīchǎng | N | airport | 063 |

145	机会	jīhuì	N	chance	102
146	鸡肉	jīròu	N	chicken	072
147	基地	jīdì	N	base	103
148	急	jí	Adj	hurried	063
149	集合	jíhé	V	to gather	103
150	忌口	jì kǒu	V//O	to avoid certain food	072
151	季节	jìjié	N	season	092
152	家	jiā	N	family, home	083
153	家乡	jiāxiāng	N	hometown	083
154	见面	jiàn miàn	V//O	to meet	082
155	建	jiàn	V	to build	103
156	健康	jiànkāng	Adj	healthy	102
157	健身	jiànshēn	V	to keep fit	101
158	健身房	jiànshēnfáng	N	gymnasium	101
159	讲评	jiǎngpíng	V	to comment	103
160	教练	jiàoliàn	N	coach	103
161	接	jiē	V	to meet, to pick up	063
162	接	jiē	V	to receive	082
163	结束	jiéshù	V	to end	103
164	近	jìn	Adj	near	061
165	景点	jǐngdiǎn	N	scenic spot	093
166	交	jiāo	V	to pay	062
167	酒	jiǔ	N	wine	062
168	举办	jǔbàn	V	to hold	091
169	俱乐部	jùlèbù	N	club	102
170	聚会	jùhuì	V/N	to get together; get-together, party	083

K

171	咖啡厅	kāfēitīng	N	cafe	082
172	卡	kǎ	N	card	102
173	卡拉OK	kǎlā-OK		karaoke	103
174	开	kāi	V	to blossom	092
175	开	kāi	V	to begin, to start	102
176	可	kě	Adv	really	091
177	课程	kèchéng	N	course	103
178	空气	kōngqì	N	air	093
179	空儿	kòngr	N	free time	082
180	口号	kǒuhào	N	slogan	103
181	款	kuǎn	M	(a measure word) kind, style	062

L

182	垃圾	lājī	N	garbage	103
183	辣	là	Adj	hot, spicy	072
184	篮球	lánqiú	N	basketball	101
185	浪漫	làngmàn	Adj	romantic	083
186	冷	lěng	Adj	cold	092
187	离	lí	V	to be away from	063
188	礼品	lǐpǐn	N	gift, present	091
189	礼物	lǐwù	N	gift	083
190	厉害	lìhai	Adj	awesome	102
191	练习	liànxí	V/N	to practice; exercise	102
192	凉快	liángkuai	Adj	cool	093
193	零下	língxià	N	below zero	093
194	留言	liú yán	V//O	to leave a message	081
195	流行	liúxíng	V	to be popular	071

196	楼	lóu	N	floor, storey	062
197	路口	lùkǒu	N	crossing, intersection	061
198	旅行	lǚxíng	V	to travel, to tour	101
199	旅游	lǚyóu	V	to travel	093
200	绿	lǜ	Adj	green	092
201	乱	luàn	Adj	messy	103

M

202	马路	mǎlù	N	street, road	061
203	嘛	ma	MdPt	*a modal particle expressing that the situation is obvious*	072
204	买单	mǎidān	V	to pay the bill	072
205	美	měi	Adj	beautiful	093
206	闷	mēn	Adj	stuffy, muggy	092
207	门口	ménkǒu	N	doorway, entrance, gate	103
208	米	mǐ	M	meter	101
209	米饭	mǐfàn	N	cooked rice	072
210	秘书	mìshū	N	secretary	081
211	目前	mùqián	N	at present	102

N

212	哪里	nǎli	Pr	not really	102
213	那边	nàbiān	Pr	there	062
214	那儿	nàr	Pr	there	071
215	南边	nánbian	N	south	061
216	南门	nánmén	N	south gate	071
217	嗯	ǹg	Int	*expressing a positive answer*	083
218	年假	niánjià	N	annual leave	091
219	牛肉	niúròu	N	beef	072

220	暖和	nuǎnhuo	Adj	warm	093

P

221	爬山	pá shān	V O	to climb a mountain	103
222	牌子	páizi	N	brand	062
223	攀岩	pānyán	V	to climb the rock	103
224	旁边	pángbiān	N	side, adjacent place	062
225	啤酒	píjiǔ	N	beer	072
226	漂亮	piàoliang	Adj	beautiful	092
227	平均	píngjūn	Adj	average	093
228	瓶	píng	N	bottle	072
229	破费	pòfèi	V	to go to such expense	072

Q

230	前	qián	N	front	061
231	切	qiē	V	to cut	102
232	亲自	qīnzì	Adv	in person	083
233	晴天	qíngtiān	N	sunny day	091
234	请客	qǐng kè	V//O	to invite sb. to dinner	072
235	秋天	qiūtiān	N	autumn	092
236	球	qiú	N	ball	102
237	球包	qiúbāo	N	golf bag	102
238	球场	qiúchǎng	N	course	102
239	球童	qiútóng	N	caddy	102
240	球友	qiúyǒu	N	golfer	102
241	取	qǔ	V	to get, to take	063
242	确定	quèdìng	V	to decide	103

R

243	让	ràng	V	to allow, to let	083
244	热	rè	Adj	hot	092
245	热身	rèshēn	V	to warm up	103
246	人力	rénlì	N	manpower	102
247	人们	rénmen	N	people	093
248	肉	ròu	N	meat	072
249	如何	rúhé	Pr	how	102
250	入住	rùzhù	V	to check in	103

S

251	沙发	shāfā	N	sofa	101
252	沙坑	shākēng	N	bunker	102
253	山地	shāndì	N	hilly area	102
254	擅自	shànzì	Adv	without prior consent	103
255	上	shang	N	above, over, on top of, on the surface of	062
256	身体	shēntǐ	N	body	101
257	生日	shēngrì	N	birthday	083
258	十一	Shí-Yī	N	National Day	093
259	十一月	shíyīyuè	N	November	092
260	时间	shíjiān	N	time	063
261	事项	shìxiàng	N	item	103
262	收	shōu	V	to bring to an end, to stop	103
263	收银台	shōuyíntái	N	checkout counter, cashier	062
264	手感	shǒugǎn	N	the feel of touching	102
265	手机	shǒujī	N	mobile phone	083
266	舒服	shūfu	Adj	comfortable	091

267	蔬菜	shūcài	N	vegetable	072
268	属于	shǔyú	V	to belong to	102
269	树叶	shùyè	N	leaf	092
270	水上	shuǐshàng	N	aquatic	103
271	司机	sījī	N	driver	063
272	死	sǐ	Adj	extremely, to death	091
273	四季	sìjì	N	four seasons	093
274	送	sòng	V	to send, to give	091
275	酸	suān	Adj	sour	072
276	随便	suí biàn	V//O	to do as one likes	083

T

277	谈	tán	V	to talk	082
278	汤	tāng	N	soup	072
279	踢	tī	V	to kick, to play	101
280	体育	tǐyù	N	sports	101
281	天公作美	tiāngōng zuòměi	IE	Heaven is cooperative	091
282	天气	tiānqì	N	weather	091
283	天然	tiānrán	Adj	natural	102
284	甜	tián	Adj	sweet	072
285	条	tiáo	M	*a measure word*	072
286	跳水	tiàoshuǐ	V	to dive	103
287	听说	tīngshuō	V	to hear of	092
288	停	tíng	V	to stop	063
289	通过	tōngguò	Prep	through	102
290	推	tuī	V	to push	102
291	推出	tuīchū	V	to promote	062
292	推荐	tuījiàn	V	to recommend	102

293	拓展	tuòzhǎn	V	to expand	102

W

294	哇	wa	MdPt	*a modal particle*	071
295	完	wán	V	to finish	091
296	晚餐	wǎncān	N	supper, dinner	103
297	晚会	wǎnhuì	N	party	103
298	碗	wǎn	N	bowl	072
299	往	wǎng	Prep	to, towards	061
300	忘	wàng	V	to forget	063
301	旺季	wàngjì	N	busy season	093
302	为	wèi	Prep	for	102
303	未来	wèilái	N	in the future	091
304	喂	wèi	Int	hello (used when making a phone call)	081
305	温度	wēndù	N	temperature	091
306	问题	wèntí	N	problem	063
307	午餐	wǔcān	N	lunch	103
308	午休	wǔxiū	V	to take a noon break	103
309	物美价廉	wù měi jià lián		of excellent quality and resonable price	062

X

310	喜欢	xǐhuan	V	to like	072
311	细节	xìjié	N	detail	082
312	下	xià	N	below, down, underneath	062
313	下	xià	N	next	072
314	下厨	xià chú	V O	to cook	083
315	夏天	xiàtiān	N	summer	092

316	现场	xiànchǎng	N	scene	091
317	羡慕	xiànmù	V	to envy	101
318	项目	xiàngmù	N	program	103
319	心情	xīnqíng	N	mood	102
320	信心	xìnxīn	N	confidence	102
321	行程	xíngchéng	N	travel route, itinerary	103
322	行动	xíngdòng	V/N	to act; action	103
323	行李	xíngli	N	luggage	063
324	型	xíng	N	model	102
325	休	xiū	V	to have one's vacation	091
326	选	xuǎn	V	to choose, to select	103
327	雪	xuě	N	snow	092
328	训练	xùnliàn	V	to train	102

Y

329	压力	yālì	N	pressure	102
330	羊肉	yángròu	N	mutton	072
331	阳光	yángguāng	N	sunshine	102
332	氧吧	yǎngbā	N	oxygen bar	102
333	要求	yāoqiú	V/N	to request; request	103
334	野外	yěwài	Adj	field, outdoor	103
335	一会儿	yíhuìr	Q	a little while	082
336	一样	yíyàng	Adj	same	092
337	已经	yǐjīng	Adv	already	063
338	以外	yǐwài	N	beyond, outside	101
339	一起	yìqǐ	Adv	together	072
340	一些	yìxiē	Q	some	091
341	一直	yìzhí	Adv	straight	061

342	音乐	yīnyuè	N	music	101
343	饮料	yǐnliào	N	drink, beverage	072
344	应该	yīnggāi	OpV	should, ought to	083
345	营	yíng	N	camp	103
346	优势	yōushì	N	advantage	102
347	油腻	yóunì	Adj	oily, greasy	072
348	游客	yóukè	N	tourist	093
349	游泳	yóuyǒng	V	to swim	101
350	右	yòu	N	right	062
351	鱼	yú	N	fish	072
352	羽绒服	yǔróngfú	N	down coat	092
353	雨水	yǔshuǐ	N	rainwater	093
354	预报	yùbào	V	to forecast	091
355	预订	yùdìng	V	to reserve	071
356	预约	yùyuē	V	to reserve	102
357	员工	yuángōng	N	employee, staff	091
358	远	yuǎn	Adj	far	063
359	约	yuē	V	to date	102
360	越…… 越……	yuè…… yuè……		more…more…	102
361	越来越	yuè lái yuè		more and more	093
362	运动	yùndòng	V/N	to exercise; sport	101
363	运动服	yùndòngfú	N	sports suit / wear	103
364	运动鞋	yùndòngxié	N	gym shoes	103

Z

365	在	zài	V	to exist, to be, to lie	061
366	早餐	zǎocān	N	breakfast	103

367	帐篷	zhàngpeng	N	tent	103
368	折	zhé	N	discount	071
369	这么	zhème	Pr	so, such, this way, like this	082
370	这儿	zhèr	Pr	here	062
371	这样	zhèyàng	Pr	this way	083
372	着	zhe	AP	*an aspect particle*	062
373	正	zhèng	Adv	*indicating an action or state is going on*	062
374	正好	zhènghǎo	Adv	happen to, just	082
375	正在	zhèngzài	Adv	in the process of	071
376	正宗	zhèngzōng	Adj	authentic	072
377	只	zhǐ	Adv	only, just	101
378	质量	zhìliàng	N	quality	093
379	中	zhōng	N	during	093
380	钟头	zhōngtóu	N	hour	101
381	周六	zhōuliù	N	Saturday	102
382	周日	zhōurì	N	Sunday	103
383	周五	zhōuwǔ	N	Friday	103
384	猪肉	zhūròu	N	pork	072
385	主食	zhǔshí	N	staple food	072
386	注意	zhùyì	V	to pay attention to	103
387	着装	zhuózhuāng	V/N	to wear (clothes, etc.); clothing	103
388	资源	zīyuán	N	resource	102
389	自己	zìjǐ	Pr	oneself	062
390	总结	zǒngjié	V	to summarize	103
391	总经理	zǒngjīnglǐ	N	general manager	081
392	租	zū	V	to rent	083
393	足球	zúqiú	N	football	101

394	组	zǔ	N	group	103
395	最	zuì	Adv	most	083
396	左	zuǒ	N	left	061
397	做客	zuò kè	V//O	to be a guest	083

专有名词
Proper Nouns

G				
1	工体北路	Gōngtǐ Běilù	name of a road (Gongti is the abbreviation of the Worker's Gymnasium.)	082
H				
2	怀柔	Huáiróu	suburban district in the northeast of Beijing	103
J				
3	家乐福	Jiālèfú	Carrefour	061
4	金龙公司	Jīnlóng Gōngsī	name of a company	081
K				
5	凯宾斯基饭店	Kǎibīnsījī Fàndiàn	Kempinski Hotel	072
L				
6	林	Lín	a surname	081
7	林琳	Lín Lín	name of a person	082

S				
8	双鱼座	Shuāngyú Zuò	Pisces	083
W				
9	王府井大街	Wángfǔjǐng Dàjiē	Wangfujing Street	091
10	沃尔玛	Wò'ěrmǎ	Walmart	061
X				
11	香山	Xiāng Shān	mountain in Beijing	092
Z				
12	中秋节	Zhōngqiū Jié	the Mid-Autumn Festival	091

汉语1000常用字
1000 Frequently Used Chinese Characters

部首　　　笔画数　　　笔顺
Radical　Number of strokes　Stroke order

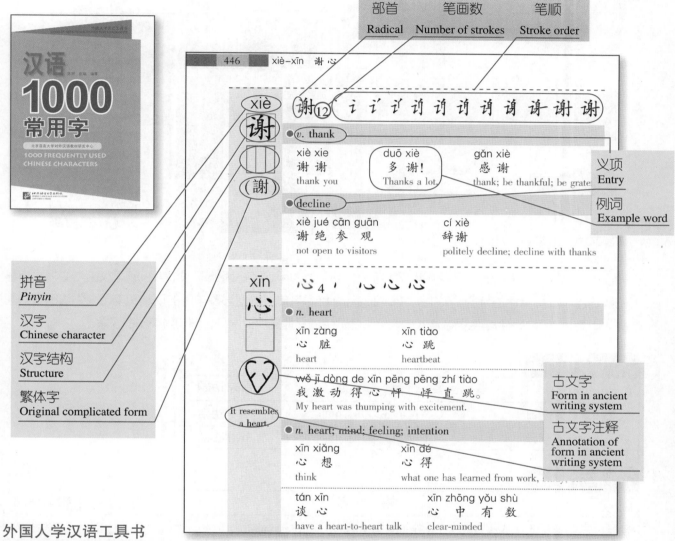

义项
Entry

例词
Example word

古文字
Form in ancient writing system

古文字注释
Annotation of form in ancient writing system

拼音
Pinyin

汉字
Chinese character

汉字结构
Structure

繁体字
Original complicated form

外国人学汉语工具书
CHINESE REFERENCE SERIES FOR FOREIGNERS

- 收录最常用汉字1000个。

  With 1000 most frequently used Chinese characters

- 例词、例句简单实用，贴近生活。

  With example words and sentences that are simple, practical and close to life

- 提供音序、笔画、部首多种检字法，便于检索。

  With multiple indexing systems to help locate the characters, including phonetic indexing, stroke indexing and radical indexing

ISBN 978-7-5619-2703-8

定价：55.00元

实用汉语分级阅读丛书
Step-by-Step Chinese Reading for Practical Purposes

崔永华　总主编

● **开本：**小16开
● **注释文种：**英文/韩文/日文

　　本套丛书根据《汉语水平词汇与汉字等级大纲》分为甲、乙、丙、丁四个等级，可以由学生根据自己的汉语水平选择合适的分册。书中的文章多选自报纸和杂志，内容涉及中国的现状和中国人生活的方方面面。本套丛书可以帮助学生更好地认读汉字、识记生词，提高汉语水平，增加对中国的了解。

甲级读本 Level 1

书　　名		相关话题
我在中国的那些日子	When I was in China	留学生活
我在中国的那些日子2	When I was in China 2	留学生活

乙级读本 Level 2

书　　名		相关话题
从"一窍不通"到"胸有成竹"	From a Layman to a Professional	成语故事
从"坐井观天"到"鹏程万里"	From the Bottom to the Top	成语故事
中国人有趣的实话实说	Chinese People Like to Speak the Truth	中国人
中国人喜欢跳舞	Chinese People Like to Dance	中国事
中国的"负翁"越来越多	There Are More and More Indebted Persons in China	中国经济
中国教育跟西方不一样	China's Education is Different from that of Western Countries	中国教育
我当上了中国女婿	I Married a Chinese Girl	中国情感
砍价是一种享受	Bargaining Is a Kind of Enjoyment	生活感悟
我是世界上最幽默的人	I'm the Most Humorous Person in the World	语言·文化

丙级读本 Level 3

书　　名		相关话题
用明天的钱，实现今天的梦	Use Tomorrow's Money to Fulfil Today's Dream	中国经济·生活